Communicating to Lead and Motivate

Communicating to Lead and Motivate

William C. Sharbrough

BUSINESS EXPERT PRESS

Communicating to Lead and Motivate

First published in 2017 by
Business Expert Press, LLC
222 East 46th Street, New York, NY 10017
www.businessexpertpress.com

ISBN-13: 978-1-60649-524-7 (paperback)
ISBN-13: 978-1-60649-525-4 (e-book)

Business Expert Press Corporate Communication Collection

Collection ISSN: 2156-8162 (print)
Collection ISSN: 2156-8170 (electronic)

Cover and interior design by Exeter Premedia Services Private Ltd., Chennai, India

First edition: 2017

10 9 8 7 6 5 4 3 2 1

Printed in the United States of America.

Abstract

Effective leaders lead by communicating. It is through communication that leadership is enacted as leaders influence followers to behave in ways that achieve the leader's and the organization's goals. This book applies leadership theory and research to communication in ways that are easily understood and can be applied to any situation where individuals find themselves in a leadership position in an organization whether as a front-line or top-level leader.

The book begins with a basic explanation of the leadership process and how leaders express their vision. It then looks at how leaders can create positive relationships with followers that pay off in effective performance. Next, the book investigates how leaders motivate their followers by creating follower self-efficacy, trust, and valued rewards. Then, the focus changes to the specific types of messages a leader can use to motivate followers. Leading is about change, so the book next looks at ways effective leaders communicate in leading change in organizations and at how the changing workforce is effecting how effective leaders communicate with the new workforce.

Keywords

change, communication, direction-giving, diversity, emotions, empathy, goals, leaders, leadership, listening, messages, organizational meaning, performance, rewards, self-efficacy, trust, vision

Contents

Acknowledgments

Effective leadership is enacted through communicating as leaders influence followers to behave in ways that achieve the leader's and the organization's goals. This book applies leadership theory and research to communication in ways that are easily understood and can be applied to any situation where individuals find themselves in a leadership position in an organization whether as a front-line or top-level leader. In addition to years of academic study of management, leadership and communication, this book is based on my over 40 years of experience as a leader and a follower.

I could not have written this book without the encouragement, help, and support of many people, including all the people I've worked for or supervised over the years. To all of them, thank you. I'm sure there are others that deserve my thanks and appreciation that I won't recognize here; to them, I apologize, and thank you, as well. Then there are those that truly stand out.

First among those that deserve my thanks is Debbie DuFrene, my friend and editor. Debbie deserves credit for pushing me to write this book in the first place, and then having the patience to endure my less than rapid pace. She has an immense amount of patience and encouragement that kept me going through the times when I got distracted with life's other tasks. Debbie is an excellent editor, who helped me with stylistic issues and was a tireless editor, rapidly turning around drafts until we got them right. Thank you, Debbie.

My mother and father deserve thanks for the love and encouragement they gave me to reach out to new ideas and places far from the small farm town where I grew up. Their emotional and financial support through college and beyond has helped me through the difficult times. I know my Mom would be proud of her son and this accomplishment. My Dad still provides an example of everyday hard work that leads to success. He will be one of the first to get a copy of this book. The roots that he planted and nourished will always be there for me and my family.

Not everyone has in-laws that provide an example of what your life is to be. They were college people, with Tom a professor and Jan a college staffer and wife. They modeled the way for me to follow the academic life, and their example has been a good one. Thanks to them as well.

Most of all, my wife, Dana, deserves thanks for the love, encouragement, patience, and emotional support she has provided. She's given me all these things and three wonderful children. All of them deserve my thanks, and giving me people that I wanted to be a leader and to "set the example" for.

To the citadel for providing sabbatical support which helped along the way, for friends who mean so much, and to all the leaders and followers I have learned from and practiced on over the years, thank you.

—William C. Sharbrough III

CHAPTER 1

Leaders Communicate a Vision

Effective leaders lead by communicating. As noted by Conger more than 20 years ago, "The era of managing [leading] by dictate is ending and is being replaced by an era of managing [leading] by inspiration." He further states that the most important skill needed by leaders is the ability to create messages that are "motivational."[1] In 2003, a researcher said, "Of all leadership behaviors, the ability to communicate may be the most important. Communication lays the foundation for leading others."[2]

In the decade since, communication has become even more critical to effective leadership. Changing expectations, increased levels of employee empowerment, and the expanding use of teams have all contributed to changes in the ways that effective leaders lead. As leaders influence followers to behave in ways that achieve the organization's and leader's goals, leadership occurs. This book applies both communication theory and research and leadership theory and research to leaders and the process of leadership in ways that are easily understood and applied to any situation or organizational level where you may find yourself.

Research consistently shows that when leaders communicate effectively with their followers, performance and job satisfaction increase. Other positive outcomes are decreased absenteeism and turnover. In today's hectic and rapidly evolving environment, effective leader communication also leads to increased follower self-efficacy, organizational commitment, and innovation.[3] All of these positive outcomes occur with few, if any, negative side effects and are critical to organizational effectiveness.

Leadership Is...

Leadership, as noted by James MacGregor Burns, "is one of the most observed and least understood phenomena on earth."[4] The various definitions of leadership and related research can be categorized according to four themes: leader traits, leader influence (use of power), leader behaviors, and leader–follower interactions. Typical definitions of leadership may be summarized as "getting people to do something they wouldn't do by themselves." While physical traits such as fitness, attractiveness, etc., seem to have little impact on leader effectiveness, psychological traits such as extroversion, willingness to communicate, emotional intelligence, etc., have been associated with effective leadership.[5]

Leader behaviors focus on either an emphasis on the followers' needs or accomplishing the task. The role of power and influence are the subject of much research, while the nature of the leader–follower interactions is a relatively new branch of research in leadership. Communication is implicit in most of the research and definitions of leadership. However, it is only in the past 25 years or so that scholars have begun to investigate the specific role of communication in leadership.

This book focuses on how leaders use communication in their efforts to influence followers. Leaders not only have to give directions but also have to explain and convince followers of the reason for those directions. While leaders may communicate with their followers through written messages (paper, e-mails, texts, etc.), the majority and preferred method of leader communication is oral (face-to-face, telephone, videoconferencing, etc.). The emphasis of the book is on oral communication unless otherwise noted. However, all guidance provided applies equally to written as well as spoken messages by leaders.

As noted, leadership is one of the most studied concepts in the literature of organizations, though there is little agreement on its definition or what constitutes effectiveness. Bennis and Nanus stated in 1985 that "decades of academic analysis have given us more than 340 definitions of leadership.[6]

However, there are some common themes among the many definitions: (1) leader traits, (2) the exercise of influence or power, (3) leader behaviors/the importance of followers, and (4) leader–follower collaboration. All four themes implicitly involve communication. This leads to a communication-based definition of leadership as

As the authors note, "Leadership shares all the features of human communication. . . . First, leaders use symbols to create reality . . . through language, stories, and rituals. . . . Second, leaders communicate about the past, present, and future, to create a desirable vision. . . . Third, leaders make conscious use of symbols to reach their goals."[7] Further, effective leaders are good listeners who apply listening skills in their relationships with their followers.

Thus, leaders lead by communicating with followers and creating messages directed at those followers which influence their behavior in the leader's desired direction. Leaders must communicate the mission of the organization to followers, framing it in terms that followers can easily understand. Then, they must communicate the vision or end state that the followers have to work toward to achieve both the leader's and organization's goals.

In fact, the higher the level of responsibility, the more the leader's time and effort is spent in communicating and the higher is the demand for communication competence. Leaders who are perceived as competent communicators by their followers share and respond to information in a timely manner, actively listen to others' points of view, communicate clearly and succinctly to all levels of the organization, and use differing communication channels.[8] Leader communication competence can include clarity of expression, situation-appropriate language usage, and job-specific communication skills (skills related to customer service, sales, human resources, etc.). Research has indicated that communication competence is a good predictor of overall leader performance.[9]

While early research on physical leader traits has had little support, more recent approaches have focused on behavioral traits. Traits such as extroversion, willingness to communicate, impression management, emotional intelligence, are associated with effective leadership and reflect aspects of communication.

The Role of Vision

Much of the current focus of leadership theory and practice focuses on "vision." Leaders must have a vision of the state or place they want their followers to move to or attain. Whether this vision is as complex as one of societal change or as simple as increasing productivity by two percent, effective leaders must be able to communicate this vision to their followers in a clear and convincing way that followers can both understand and work to achieve. While "vision" implies looking into the distant future at the top of organizations, vision can be as simple as knowing and expressing what needs to be done to accomplish small tasks on the front lines of the organization. A *Harvard Business Review* article noted that effective vision routinely has an "almost mundane quality" based on current ideas.[10] Regardless of its complexity, the leader must express that vision to followers in a clear and compelling way. Leaders must also choose symbolic words and language that give emotional power to their message, creating a clear sense of direction for the organization and its members.

To frame the vision or leadership message effectively, leaders should organize their thoughts and choose words that clearly and vividly lay out what is to be accomplished, creating a "map for action"[11] and generating "energized behavior"[12] in the followers. The leader may also tell stories about the organization, its founders, and its past, or other organizations and people to lay out the vision and make it concrete for followers. These stories and rituals may also describe the values and traditions of the organization and its culture, which form the basis for the organization's mission and the leader's vision.

These stories, and the organizational rituals that sometimes accompany them, also help the leader create the emotional power needed to motivate followers. One example would be the ritualistic way that Steve Jobs and Apple introduced new products. Even after his death, Apple follows the same format/ritual to introduce their new products, continuing the tone and culture of leadership at Apple Corporation.

Effective leaders choose metaphors and analogies to give their messages emotional strength. Clearly, many business leaders see their task as a battle, a war to be won, "a hill to be taken," etc. and encourage the widespread use of military-related language in business. Likewise, others see their organizations as competitors and use sports analogies such as "in overtime," "major league," etc. to accomplish the same purpose. In today's rapidly changing, highly technological business environment, we are hearing more stories, analogies, and metaphors from the world of computers and cyberspace ("multitasking," "in the cloud," etc.). Such language choice can help leaders define the vision and culture for their organizations.

Other traditional speech techniques may also be used to help build the emotional power that leaders need.[13] Repetition, rhythm, and alliteration (all in the toolboxes of religious and political leaders) can also aid a leader in building followers' emotional commitment to the vision. While beyond the scope of this book, you may want to investigate and practice using these techniques as well.

To sum up, leaders influence others to follow by communicating clear directions toward a compelling vision of a more positive situation or objective. The effective communication of this vision or message motivates followers so they exert energy toward achieving this objective. A leader who cannot successfully communicate, may have a vision, but that vision is just a hallucination. Followers will not follow and the leader cannot lead.

A Preview

After a brief introduction to the concept of leadership as communication and the role of vision in this chapter, the following chapters focus on followers, for leading requires followers. Chapter 2 looks at the relationships between leaders and followers and at how leaders can create positive relationships that pay off in effective performance.

Chapter 3 continues to explore these relationships through effective listening. Listening to followers helps leaders make better decisions and develop more positive relationships.

Chapter 4 explores what leader actions and behaviors motivate followers. Creating follower self-efficacy and trust and offering valued rewards are keys to successful leadership. This chapter gives specific advice to leaders concerning how to create positive expectations.

Leaders use a variety of messages to motivate followers to perform effectively, as examined in Chapter 5. Message types include giving directions, creating meaning, and expressing empathy. The chapter introduces the concept of motivating language (ML) and presents a brief review of the research that indicates the positive impact of using ML on a variety of performance-related variables. The bulk of the chapter explains the kinds of messages that leaders use to motivate followers.

While not all leaders have to lead changes in their organizations, when they do, the changes may be the most difficult task they face. On a smaller scale, all leadership is about change. Chapter 6 looks at ways effective leaders communicate in leading change in their organizations. Specifically, the chapter discusses the reasons that followers may resist changes and the steps required to lead a successful change.

Chapter 7 focuses on concepts and strategies related to leading a group of culturally diverse followers. It begins by discussing today's diverse workforce and how it has changed over the past several years. It then looks at different aspects of diversity and how they may impact a leader's communication efforts. The chapter concludes with techniques for capitalizing on the diversity of your work group to be a more effective leader.

The final chapter reviews the different ways that leaders communicate and gives guidance for practicing effective leader communication. Several appendices provide resource materials and activities that leaders can use to strengthen communication with their followers.

CHAPTER 2

Leadership Is About Relationships

Being a leader implies that there is at least one person who acts as a follower and there may be many. A leader's followers could range from one or two individuals who report directly to the leader to all the members of a Fortune 500–sized organization below the CEO level. However, leadership is very personal, and a good way to view being a leader is at the one-on-one or leader–follower level, and the relationship between the leader and follower. Pete Anderson, director of Operations, Advanced Airplane Programs at Gulfstream Inc., in a recent talk to a group of college seniors, began by saying that "leadership is about relationships." Two of the most important factors in leader–follower relationships are trust and consideration.

Earning Trust

Leaders must be able to trust their followers, just as followers must be able to trust their leaders. However, trust must be developed or earned as relationships grow between a leader and a follower. A leader's clear, open, and fair communication with followers is a good starting place for developing trust.

Clear. While clear communication may seem as simple as "saying what you mean/meaning what you say," it also involves choosing the right words and messages to ensure that followers understand what the leader wants them to do. By learning about the background and experience of each follower, the leader can make more effective choices in framing messages that are clear and understandable to the follower.

An effective leader will use a different level of specificity in giving directions to a new, fresh-out-of-college employee than when giving directions to a 20-year veteran of the organization. If an organization has its own way of accomplishing a particular task, an effective leader will spend time explaining "how we do it" to a new employee who has come from a different organization in the same industry.

When you use e-mails or other written message forms to communicate with followers, it's a good idea to carefully proofread those messages before sending them. When proofreading, try to envision the message from the viewpoint of the follower, choosing words and phrases that are familiar to the follower and avoiding any misleading or confusing jargon.

It is rumored that both Napoleon and General Ulysses S. Grant kept a "dumb" lieutenant on staff to proofread any written orders the generals sent to their troops. If that lieutenant could understand the order, the generals knew that the rest of the officers would be able to understand it. While keeping "dumb" employees on staff is not a great idea, getting an associate to proofread messages before they are "published" to the people who will implement them is a good rule of thumb.

To make sure your oral messages are clear, have followers paraphrase those messages back to you. As a leader, you will have to use tact in eliciting this feedback. Effective leaders try to communicate openly, fairly, and consistently with their followers. They are considerate of their followers and communicate their decisions and actions with integrity.

Open. Unless there are valid (competitive secrecy or confidentiality) reasons, it is rarely a good idea to withhold job- or organization-related information from followers. Followers can make better decisions and need less supervision when they understand how their work fits into the overall goal of the organization. A leader who tactfully expresses emotions (either positive or negative) in response to a follower's actions can also increase the level of trust the follower has in the leader.

Fair and consistent. Not only do leaders have to be clear and open in their communication, they also must be fair and consistent in their behavior with the followers. Followers need to know that they will be treated fairly if they are to begin to trust a leader. Also, when leaders are consistent in their dealings with followers, followers can expect them to continue to act in that manner. This makes it easier for followers to trust the leader because they can understand expectations and guide their own efforts and performance.

Another way of thinking about consistency is for leaders to "lead by example" or "walk the talk." While these phrases can be seen as clichés, they express the idea that a leader's behavior communicates just as words do. It is unrealistic to expect followers to behave as the leader directs when the leader's behavior is inconsistent with the stated expectations.

Trusting your followers is as important in the leader–follower relationship as having the followers trust you as the leader. To enhance trust, a follower must also communicate clearly and openly with the leader. While effective leaders "lead by example," effective (and trusted) followers consistently meet the leader's stated performance expectations and keep their leaders informed at all times. Table 2.1 includes additional suggestions for building trust.

As leaders and followers learn to trust each other, they will communicate more effectively, work toward organizational goals with more enthusiasm, and develop more positive relationships with each other. As they

Table 2.1 Building trust

Tell the truth, even when it hurts you.
Keep your promises.
Commit to values that respect others.
Be known for having high standards of integrity.
Don't let ambition get in the way of fairness and honesty.

Adapted from Williams (2007); Neubert and Dyck (2014).

communicate more fully and effectively with each other, "they feel better and accomplish more, and the organization prospers."[1]

Being Considerate

As leaders and followers communicate more fully and effectively, they begin to know and understand each other on a personal as well as formal organizational level. This understanding allows the leader to recognize the individual needs, desires, and ambitions of followers and take these things into account when leading them as individuals.

For instance, if a follower has confidence issues, the leader may want to provide extra feedback. Conversely, followers with extensive on-the-job experience may require less supervision than less experienced followers. Recognizing that followers are individuals with differing needs, desires, work–life situations, and ambitions is the first step in being considerate. While a leader cannot always take such issues into account in making decisions, followers appreciate such efforts and will react more favorably toward a leader who tries to be considerate. Followers view this consideration as an indication that the leader cares about them, and they will be more likely to trust the leader.

Developing Relationships

Most leadership theory and research concentrates on the leader, considers traits and behaviors of the leader, and assumes that leaders lead all their followers in the same way. However, one widely researched and accepted theory centers on the relationship between the leader and the follower. The essential idea behind the Leader-Member Exchange (LMX) Theory is that the more positive the relationship between a leader and follower, the more effective leadership will be. Research indicates that positive leader–follower relationships lead to improved performance, satisfaction, reduced turnover, and other positive worker outcomes.[2]

The relationship between a leader and follower frequently advances through three stages of development. In the first, leaders and followers are *strangers*. As the relationship develops, it moves to the point that the leader and follower are *acquaintances*. When the relationship is fully developed, it can be described as a *mature partnership*.[3] Most people have been through these stages of relationships in a variety of contexts in both personal and organizational settings. The explanations that follow focus on the relationship between leaders and followers.

Stage 1: Strangers. In this first stage, the leader and follower are essentially strangers and test each other to see what is expected. The interactions between leader and follower adhere to the formal rules of the employment/contractual roles. The relationship is essentially impersonal, and expectations of both the leader and follower mirror the job description. Leaders give orders/make requests and followers comply to achieve their own goals as members of the organization, such as receiving a paycheck. Followers who seek feedback about ways to improve performance and better understand their position signal they are interested in moving to a more positive relationship with the leader, and leaders should be quick to provide effective feedback.[4]

Stage 2: Acquaintances. As leaders and followers get to know each other, they behave more like acquaintances as they move into the second stage of the leader–follower relationship. Trust, loyalty, and respect for each other begin to develop. Fairness of the leader is critical during this stage as it leads to increased commitment to the leader from followers. Followers will become more willing to go beyond the bare minimum, leading to potential competitive advantage for the organization.[5]

Stage 3: Partners. Some leader–follower relationships continue to develop into the third stage of the partnership. Mutual trust, respect, and obligation toward each other are high. Relationships have been tested, and both leaders and followers know they can depend on each other and are likely to do each other favors and offer assistance when needed. Essentially, both the leader and follower are connected in ways that go beyond the formal work relationship. This relationship allows them to offer both criticism and support to each other and produces positive outcomes for the leader and follower as well as the organization.[6]

Early research in LMX theory focused on the differences in exchanges (communication relationships) between leaders and followers in stages 1 and 2 as just described. Later research expanded to include stage 3 and provides advice on how a leader can move relationships beyond stage 1 (an out-group) to more productive and satisfying stage 2 and 3 relationships (in-groups) by looking for ways to increase trust and respect with all members of the work group. One group of authors noted:

Effective leadership occurs when the communication of leaders and [followers] is characterized by mutual trust, respect, and commitment.[7]

Growing the In-Group: Building Relationships

What should you, as a leader, do to build positive relationships with your followers? First, it is important to recognize that a leader has a unique relationship with each follower, and effective leaders work to move all relationships beyond stage 1, increasing the size of the in-group and reducing the out-group. First impressions are surely important, and you will want to work hard to ensure that you create a positive first impression with new followers. Likewise, the leader should work hard to develop a positive first impression of a new follower.

You can apply various strategies for creating positive relationships with followers. These included getting to know followers, helping followers get to know you, offering new work opportunities to followers (empowering them), and making sure that exchanges between you and your followers are of the highest quality.

Getting to Know Your Followers

Pete Anderson, of Gulfstream Inc., emphasized the importance of knowing your followers. Knowing your follower's background helps you communicate more clearly with that follower and develop a more positive relationship. The better you know your followers, the more effective you will be in choosing the words and media to communicate various kinds of messages to them. Leaders need to know about followers' personalities, work–life interactions, experiences, and ambitions. Knowing your followers allows you to not only be more considerate of their individual situations but also be more insightful into why they behave the way they do and how you can best motivate them. Knowing your followers involves knowledge and understanding in several key areas.

Personalities. Each person has a unique personality. Personality characteristics such as extroversion, agreeableness, openness to new experiences, conscientiousness, and emotional stability[8] are different in each individual. The better you understand your own personality, the personality of your followers, and how these personalities interact, the more effectively you can lead and communicate with your followers. Taking personality tests such as the Myers-Briggs Type Indicator (www.humanmetrics.com/cgi-win/jtypes2.asp) or the Big Five Personality Test (https://www.psychologytoday.com/tests/personality/big-five-personality-test) can help you understand your own personality and help you begin to identify differences and similarities between you and your followers. As you relate more fully to the differing personalities of your followers, you can use this knowledge to develop more positive relationships.

Work–life interactions. In an ideal situation, neither the followers' nor the leader's personal and family lives would impact the work environment. However, in today's world of single-parent families, two-career couples, child care and elder care responsibilities, and social interactions, organizations are significantly impacted by what workers experience away from the workplace. By learning about the outside-of-work situations of your followers, you can better understand how to offer assistance, support, and care that can improve the quality of the relationship between you and your followers. Likewise, the more followers know about the personal and family life of the leader, the better they can understand their impact on the leader.

Experiences. Knowing the kinds of experiences your followers have had can also aid in developing relationships. Individuals are a product of their life experiences, and as Leman and Pentak point out, understanding a follower's experiences is key to knowing how to best use that follower's skills and abilities, getting the most out of the follower, and helping followers reach their own potential.[9] The leader learns where the follower can best serve the organization, and followers learn that they can count on the leader to put them in positions where they will be successful. Knowing and utilizing the experiences of followers in this way will be appreciated and will lead to stronger relationships.

Ambitions. Recognizing and helping followers achieve their ambitions will surely aid in developing a positive relationship between the leader and follower. First, such help creates obligations to the leader. Second, recognizing the dreams and desires of your followers communicates that you care about the follower as a person, not just as an employee. Third, creating opportunities for followers to stretch and grow in their work creates more capable followers and more valuable human resources for the organization. Offering followers opportunities for new roles and tasks and empowering them to make decisions and have more control over their work clearly conveys leader trust. As followers succeed, their self-confidence will increase, and trust and respect for the leader will grow as well.

Letting Them Know You

Followers want to know you. They need to know about the leader's personality, work–life interactions, and experiences. Knowing the leader aids them in better understanding why the leader behaves as she does and what motivates her. This knowledge aids followers in developing their side of a positive relationship with the leader. While what is true about getting to know followers is also true for followers getting to know leaders, there are strategies you can employ as a leader to help followers get to know you.

Most followers will pick up on a leader's personality quickly, just as the leader will recognize follower personalities quickly. However, you may find it beneficial to share some aspects of your personality with followers. For example, as the instructor/leader in my college classes, I find it beneficial to share with my class that I am not good with details. This knowledge empowers students to point out mistakes I may have made in scheduling, and so on, in time to correct them before they become a problem. Giving students the power to question the instructor seems to aid in developing a positive classroom relationship.

Sharing your personal situations with followers aids them in understanding your behavior and gives them information that not only makes you seem more human but also gives them knowledge of how to offer assistance, support, and care for you that can improve the quality of the relationship. At the same time, you should be cautious in sharing personal details as sometimes "too much information" given to others can be counterproductive to efficiency and to professional respect. Relationships are reciprocal, and sharing relevant information about one another can increase trust and make the relationship more positive.

Explaining to followers how your previous work and life experiences apply to the task and organization can be valuable to their understanding you as the leader. Additionally, informing new followers of why certain things are done the way they are in your organization assists them in becoming productive members of the organization more quickly. Followers will appreciate this sharing of information, which will deepen the relationship between you and your followers.

Knowing a leader's ambitions may not be necessary but can help to develop a relationship. Given a positive relationship already, followers can aid you in achieving your ambitions, which will surely deepen the quality of the relationship between you.

Key to Relationships

The key to developing strong, positive relationships between leaders and followers is to create and maintain **high-quality exchanges.** Effective leaders do this through their communication with followers. They focus on being clear and open. They keep followers informed so followers can make sound decisions. Effective leaders are fair and consistent in their dealings with all followers, even if they do not have strong relationships with the followers. Those leaders work to develop positive relationships with all their followers, creating an organization where all followers feel a part of the group. Keeping followers as informed about organizational happenings as possible is another tool in relationship building.

By learning who your followers are in terms of personality, life situations, experiences, and ambitions, you can communicate more effectively with them. Knowledge of one another and effective communication help increase trust and consideration between leaders and followers, which further strengthens the relationship between them.

Finally, building relationships with your peers and superiors in the organization can also impact your relationship with your followers. Much of the information you gain from these relationships can be passed along to your followers, making them more informed about the organization and its objectives. Well-informed followers will recognize the trust and respect you have for them when you share such information, and this openness will further increase the trust and respect followers have for you, making your relationship even stronger while making your followers more productive for the organization.

CHAPTER 3

Leaders Listen

Listening is one of the most important communication skills a leader can have. Listening helps leaders to understand followers and creates positive feelings between them. As noted in the previous chapter, positive relationships are key to effective leadership, and listening to followers is one way to create those relationships and to be an effective leader. Failing to listen can destroy relationships and derail a leader's efforts; it has been listed as one of the "top five reasons leaders fail, with Warren Bennis saying it is the most common reason CEOs fail."[1]

Listening goes well beyond passively "hearing" what a follower is saying to being actively involved in understanding the follower's message. As the leader, you work to comprehend the "facts, opinions, and attitudes" a follower expresses. Effective leaders give feedback and ask questions to show they are listening.[2] Most people think they are good listeners. Yet, of all that people hear, they hear 75 percent "imprecisely" and forget 75 percent of what they hear accurately after three weeks.[3] You can get an approximation of your listening ability from taking the brief quiz at the following Internet source:

> *Psychology Today* listening test:
> http://psychologytoday.tests.psychtests.com/take_test.
> php?idRegTest=3206

It is interesting that our educational systems typically include a myriad of courses in writing and speaking, but very few courses in listening. While humans may learn to hear and listen before they learn to speak, leaders need to work at being effective listeners, just as they need to work at becoming effective speakers. Most managers spend more of their time listening than speaking, reading, or writing (see Table 3.1 below), listening is a skill that few people practice effectively.[4] In fact, listening has

Table 3.1 Managerial time spent listening, speaking, reading, and writing

	Percent of time
Listening	45
Speaking	30
Reading	16
Writing	9

Source: O'Rourke (2010).

been called the "neglected skill of management."[5] Listening is particularly important for leaders because they need to understand the barriers to effective listening and the techniques that make one an effective listener.

When leaders listen effectively, especially to followers, they not only hear the complete message in words but also understand the feelings and deeper meaning behind those words.[6] One of the simplest lessons for a leader to learn in becoming an effective listener is to stop talking. However, becoming an effective listener goes well beyond that. There are several issues that make effective listening difficult. The issues listed here are some of the most common reasons that leaders (and others) listen ineffectively.

Listening Difficulties

Various things can negatively affect a leader's ability to listen.

Biases. Biases can result from such things as cultural differences, organizational roles, stereotyping, and so on. **Ethnocentrism**, the belief that our own culture is superior to others, sometimes gets in the way when listening to those from different cultures, regions, ethnic groups, and so on, and may lead to poor listening. The same problem may occur when people from different parts of the organization or those who have different professional backgrounds speak. For instance, the "geek" from IT in your meeting may have good ideas about marketing, but since he is from IT, you may automatically discount his ideas, thus failing to listen. Likewise, if a speaker has a strong accent or manner of speaking (Northeastern, Southern, West Coast, etc.), the stereotypes we have developed about people from those areas may influence our efforts to listen effectively.

Credibility. We tend to discount (sometimes with reason) what individuals who lack credibility have to say. Inexperienced employees, people who may have something to gain, people who have a poor performance record, and so on, may be perceived as less than credible sources of information. Leaders may choose to ignore or discount messages from such individuals and possibly miss important information.

Insensitive language. When people use emotionally laden, racist, sexist, or other inappropriate words in their speech, we tend to react negatively to both the individuals and their messages. A leader should not tolerate such language but should still listen carefully to the message.

Hearing only the words and facts. It is important to listen for how something is said as well as the words people use. Listening for facts is only part of effective listening. Tone of voice, facial expressions, gestures, body language, and rate of speech may all add additional important information for leaders. If you fail to notice these signals, you may miss the most important part of the message.

External distractions. A noisy plant floor, conversations in the next cubicle, lots of movement or activity around you, and other distractions can all create difficulties in listening. When alone in my office, I work with constant background music but make sure to turn it off when a coworker comes in to talk. Effective leaders try to limit distractions and create a positive environment for listening.

Emotions. If either a leader or follower is angry, upset, excited, or otherwise overstimulated by some situation, he or she may be too preoccupied to listen effectively. Effective leaders can learn to control their own emotions and help followers to control theirs so that all involved can become better listeners.

Technical language/difficult topics. It is easy to listen poorly if the message is full of technical language or the topic is perceived as difficult or uninteresting. In many such situations, ineffective listeners may choose to fake listening by engaging in nonverbal behaviors such as nodding, leaning forward, and having strong eye contact while allowing their minds to wander. Effective leaders look for ways to make a topic interesting for themselves and others, and they practice good listening by asking speakers for clarification when topics are difficult or technical.

Jumping to conclusions. It is easy to assume that you know what the speaker is trying to say and fail to listen completely and thoroughly. This is most typical when a leader and follower have worked closely together for several years. Effective leaders show patience and listen to the "whole" message before reaching conclusions.

Delivery issues. It is difficult to listen effectively when speakers have weak or monotone voices or use halting or odd pauses, filler words like uhs, you knows, and so on. Effective listeners expend the effort to listen beyond the delivery of the message.

Wasting thought speed. Our capacity for thought is much faster than our capacity to speak. Simply, we think faster than we speak. Most people can process more than 500 words a minute as listeners, but the average person speaks at a rate of 120 to 150 words per minute.[7] Effective leaders should be able to use this time difference to summarize and analyze the message and listen more completely and effectively.[8]

Improving Listening

As mentioned earlier, one of the simplest things a leader can do to improve listening is to stop talking. There are varieties of other techniques you can use to improve your listening.

Don't multitask. Effective listeners focus on the message they are hearing. Whether you are reading e-mails, listening to music, carrying on another conversation at the same time, or otherwise multitasking when someone is talking, you cannot give complete attention to any of these activities. Effective listeners cut out distractions of all kinds and give speakers their undivided attention.

Empathize. To make sure you are listening effectively, it is important to keep several iconic phrases from the 60s in mind. As a listener, if you can "walk a mile in [the speaker's] shoes" or understand "where [the speaker] is coming from," you are on your way to effective listening and complete understanding. A more sophisticated way of stating this technique is that empathizing with your speaker by trying to determine her background, experiences, emotions, and so on, will help you as the leader listen more effectively.

Ask questions/paraphrase. Psychologists should not be the only ones who use the phrase "What I hear you saying is . . ."; you can use this and similar phrases to paraphrase the speaker's message and verify that you actually understood his message as it was intended. This simple technique can also be used by leaders to make sure they are understood by tactfully asking listeners to paraphrase instructions or other messages back to the speaker.

Don't interrupt. Besides being courteous and showing respect for the follower and the message, not interrupting has other benefits. Hearing your follower's entire message before responding addresses several of the difficulties mentioned earlier. Effective leaders show patience and hear the entire message before speaking. This gives the leader time to process and create an appropriate response.

Pay attention to nonverbal messages. Is the speaker agitated, calm, excited, focused, and so on? These nonverbal behaviors, along with eye contact, tone of voice, volume, and rate of speech are all part of the message. You should observe the nonverbal messages of your followers, bearing in mind that nonverbal language is significantly influenced by culture. Additionally, leaders listen for what is NOT being said. Many times, the unspoken messages, along with the nonverbal, are as important as the spoken words.

Show interest. Effective leaders put followers at ease when they are speaking and show interest in what they are saying. This means removing the distractions already mentioned, as well as having appropriate eye contact with the follower. Effective leaders also will lean forward (if sitting) and nod in understanding to show their interest in what the follower has to say.

React to ideas, not the speaker. A speaker's credibility, use of insensitive language, poor speech or grammar habits, and emotional state can all trigger poor listening. Effective leaders make a conscious effort to listen to the ideas being expressed, listening past these kinds of distractions.

Evaluate facts and evidence. Effective leaders carefully listen to words and facts and also take advantage of thought speed to evaluate the facts and evidence. They listen for how the various parts of the message are interrelated or connect with other problems and issues they and their followers are facing.

The first step you as a leader must take to become a better listener is to recognize how poorly people listen. As noted previously, taking a listening inventory is one way to begin to identify our own poor listening habits. Additionally, asking peers and followers to evaluate your listening may also help in your self-evaluation. Then, you can identify your bad habits as a listener and consciously practice to eliminate them and replace them with more effective listening habits.

Making Sure You Are Listened to

Effective leaders also recognize that their followers also may have poor listening habits and will take steps to improve the listening habits of others.

- **Prepare the listener.** To ensure your followers are listening, you should prepare them by both controlling the environment for distractions and letting them know the importance of your message. In some situations, you may ask followers background questions to ascertain their knowledge of a situation before communicating. Obviously, followers who are well informed on a subject will need less explanation than a follower who is unfamiliar with it.
- **Choose the right time.** Effective leaders never try to communicate with their followers when either is angry, agitated, or otherwise distracted. Likewise, late Friday afternoon meetings and messages can sometimes be lost in the rush to start the weekend. Wait until a time when you know the listener can focus on your message.
- **Be organized.** Plan your message before delivering it. Make sure your message is organized so followers can easily comprehend it and how its parts fit together. Take full advantage of the important beginning and ending of a message to gain and keep attention and make sure you get your point across.
- **Be clear.** While there may be a place for ambiguity in some organizations and situations, strive to create messages that are clear and concise. While long, involved messages can be confusing to listeners, make sure to not leave anything important

out of your message. Effective leaders encourage followers' questions as one way to make sure their messages are understood. As mentioned previously, there is often value in having followers explain your message back to you to make sure they understand and you have left out nothing.

- **Choose the right pace.** Effective leaders will vary the rate of speech to fit the message, typically slowing down for more complex messages and speeding up for simpler ones.[9] A slowly delivered message will have more emphasis than a quick one. However, as in other aspects of leadership, you want to fit the pace to the follower. "Note takers" will typically need a little more time to jot down what you say than will those who don't write things down.

Effective Leaders Work at Listening

As we have discussed, effective leaders recognize the importance of listening and the difficulties involved in being a good listener. They recognize the barriers to good listening and their own bad and good listening habits, working to break the bad ones and improve the good. They also accept the fact that people are generally poor listeners, so they see that part of their job as a leader is creating a positive listening environment for their followers as well as themselves.

CHAPTER 4

Leaders Build Positive Expectations

One of the most difficult questions a leader has to answer is, "How do I get my followers to do what I want and need for them to do?" Clearly, there are no simple answers to this age-old question. How to direct the behavior of followers or how to motivate them to enact behaviors in the desired direction is a complicated process. One of the two major approaches to understanding motivation focuses on satisfying personal needs, although experts have never agreed on what these needs are or on their relative importance. The other approach highlights behaviors based on people's expectations of achieving a particular goal.[1] Combining these two approaches may help you as a leader better understand how to accomplish the task of getting followers to do what you want.

Some experts also argue that an individual cannot motivate another person, and motivation is an internal condition, that is, people motivate themselves.[2] However, from the standpoint of the leader, while you may not be able to motivate that follower, you can provide the things that will cause followers to be motivated to do the things you need and want them to do. Taking a look at motivation theories can help leaders understand the followers' needs or increase the likelihood of reaching the followers' goals. Then, regardless of whether you have motivated your followers or the followers have motivated themselves, the important thing is that the followers' behavior is in the direction and levels that you require to achieve the goals of the organization.

Introduction to Motivation Theories

The direction of behavior, the level of effort, and amount of persistence are all evidence of just how motivated a person is to satisfy some need or achieve some goal. That is, the more motivated a person is, the more he will behave in a certain way, the more effort he will put into a task, and the longer and harder he will work to achieve that task. For example, a motivated salesperson will work hard at developing a new and improved sales pitch, may increase the number of sales calls made, and may continue to work to perfect the pitch after work hours. The question for the sales manager/leader is, "Why does that salesperson put forth the energy and effort to do this?" The sales manager will then need to ask what she can do so the sales person will work toward increasing sales; essentially how can the salesperson be further motivated in the necessary direction?

As you develop relationships with followers, get to know them, their backgrounds, their needs and goals in life, and their skills and abilities, you can better understand what motivates your followers and how you can help motivate them to work toward their own and the organization's goals.

What do followers need? Either a person's needs may be inherent to being a human or they may be learned. In developed countries, we assume that basic needs such as food, clothing, shelter, and safety have been satisfied and most of our followers are not motivated to work toward gaining more of these basic staples of life. Also, many people will skip lunch to get a project done they feel is important or will risk their lives to save other people. In a longer time frame, however, while basic needs are important, they have little power to motivate. The majority of individuals may have needs for intellectual and developmental growth, for achievement and/or recognition, for being associated with others, or for power, and they are motivated to satisfy these needs. Experts have argued that some of these "needs" may be inherently human, while others are learned through our cultures, families, and life experiences.[3]

- **Growth.** An old U.S. Army recruiting advertisement stressed that in the army you could "be all that you can be." Many leaders and followers have a need to develop new skills and knowledge, take on new and more difficult tasks, assume more responsibility, and so on, as ways of growing as individuals and reaching their human potential.[4] Some people continue their education for just such reasons. Individuals

may seek new and different employment and careers as ways
to continue to grow even if they are successful yet feel they are
stagnating in their present career.

- **Achievement/recognition.** Similarly, while it may not be
  an inherent human need, many people in Western society
  develop a need to be recognized for their achievements. Many
  people feel the need to accomplish something, to be productive, and to pursue goals.[5] Some would argue that recognition
  is a stronger motivational force than bonuses and increases
  in pay. As evidence of the belief in the power of recognition,
  many organizations use "employee of the month" programs as
  a way of recognizing their best employees, give special awards
  for outstanding performance, and sponsor contests that set
  goals for employees and then recognize their achievements.

- **Being a part of a group.** The majority of humans need to
  belong to a group or at the very least have interaction with
  others. The importance of the man Friday to the main char-
  acter in the novel *Robinson Crusoe*[6] is a classic and extreme
  example of this. The power of "peer pressure" on people's
  behavior illustrates the need to fit in and be a part of a group.
  Being part of a group also gives individuals a sense of belong-
  ing and acceptance that they may not have otherwise. For
  instance, the progression of new employees from probationary
  to permanent status communicates to both the individuals
  and peers that they are accepted members of the group.

- **Power.** Some people have a need to control other people,
  influence their behavior, and/or be responsible for them.[7]
  Leaders, in particular, may have a need for power. However,
  this is surely not a universal "need" as there are some who
  will work hard to ensure that they are not put in positions
  where they have power over others. Likewise, many of us
  have worked with "control freaks" who seem excessive in their
  desire to control people and events. While "power" seems to
  have a negative connotation for many, the appropriate use
  of power is one of the important components of effective
  leadership.

How does motivation work? When trying to understand just how motivation works, one of the basic assumptions is that people's behavior is motivated both by the internal needs already discussed as well as external factors. Many researchers believe that people are motivated by the expectation of receiving some kind of reward for their efforts.[8] Broadly speaking, these rewards help satisfy the needs of followers.

One widely accepted theory of motivation that is based on this assumption is known as expectancy theory.

Expectancy theory proposes that people are motivated when they believe they can accomplish the task, they will get the reward, and the rewards for doing the task are worth the effort.[9]

So, for motivation to take place, all three of these conditions must be met:

- Followers must believe they can perform at a level necessary to complete the task the leader assigns. The leader needs to ensure that followers have the training, equipment, and supplies needed to accomplish the task.
- Followers must believe that by accomplishing the assigned task they will receive a reward. The leader MUST be able to deliver this reward to ensure motivation both in the present and for future tasks.
- The reward must be of value to the follower. The higher the value of the reward, the greater the possibility the follower will be motivated to accomplish the task.

Followers also learn that having once received a valued reward for accomplishing a task they will receive a similar reward for efforts in the future. This realization and expectation increases long-term motivation. On the other hand, punishing a follower for failing to achieve a goal serves to only decrease motivation in the future and should be avoided unless the follower's behavior is dangerous or unethical.

Putting Theory into Practice—Creating Positive Expectations

Understanding the process of motivation and being able to apply this knowledge as a leader goes well beyond understanding theory, however. While it is important to understand **how** motivation works from an intellectual standpoint, it may be more important to understand how a leader can use this knowledge to direct the behavior of followers. Let's consider some suggestions for obtaining the behavior you need from your followers and making sure they are motivated to perform.

Create a climate. Leaders should do what they can to create jobs and a work environment that provide for personal growth, group membership, and ways to recognize achievement. Mindless tasks may be necessary at times, but they will have little impact on followers' efforts to perform at an exceptional level. When the leader can create a positive work experience, most followers will appreciate it and work harder to accomplish the tasks set for them.

Know what your followers want/need. No two people have the same needs or expectations. Some individuals respond to time off, some to the proverbial "pat on the back," others to concrete rewards like prizes and bonuses, and so on. As you get to know your followers as individuals, the more you can tailor the rewards offered for performing the required tasks and effectively motivate your followers. One caveat here is that while no two followers have the same needs, the leader needs to make sure that rewards are seen by followers as fair for each of them.

Know what your followers are capable of. Not only do you need to know what your followers want, but you also need to know their skill levels, talents, and so on. Research has indicated that difficult but achievable goals have positive motivational impact while impossible goals have little, if any, positive impact on motivation or performance.[10] Thus, it is important to give followers tasks that they are capable of achieving with effort. Goals that are obviously unattainable will generally not have the desired positive effect on followers.

Clearly define tasks and performance levels. Followers need to clearly understand what they are supposed to accomplish and what level of performance will be necessary to accomplish assigned tasks.[11] Essentially, the leader must lay out the path followers need to take to reach their own goals while achieving the leader's and organization's goals. These tasks should be difficult but achievable.

Tie rewards to performance. When followers know the way to gain a reward valuable to them is to perform at a certain level or complete a specific task, they will be more likely to try to reach that target. An important task for leaders is to develop rewards that are seen as fair for the effort involved and valuable to their followers.

I once worked in a factory where the shipping department employees worked under a poorly designed incentive system. They could easily reach the maximum level they would be rewarded for on Thursday rather than at the end of the week. It was almost impossible to get them to perform beyond that level. In fact, they usually put forth just enough effort on Fridays to keep from getting bored or fired. This poorly designed reward system failed to motivate the employees to put forth any extra effort.

Leaders should always remember that they will get the behavior that they reward from their followers. If your goal is great customer service in your automobile repair shop, then you probably don't want to reward technicians for finding things wrong with customers' cars that the customer didn't know about. You may get technicians making repairs (and getting rewarded for them) that were unnecessary. You should be rewarding courtesy to customers, quick repairs, and so on.

Also, followers who work harder and perform at higher levels than others should be rewarded at a greater level than average performers. If not, they will soon learn that working harder than others is not worth it, just as the shipping department employees did.

While mistakes can be made when trying to reward performance, the benefits leaders and their organizations can gain from rewarding performance are significant.

Help followers believe in themselves. Followers who have a favorable self-concept will be helpful for the leader, but it is more important to have followers with a positive belief that they can accomplish the tasks you set for them. This strength of belief in one's own ability to complete tasks and reach goals is known as *self-efficacy*. Providing the necessary training, making sure the supplies and tools necessary are available, and so on, is important here. Offering support and encouragement to your followers as they accomplish tasks is equally important as a way to help them develop belief in their own ability to perform.

Create trust. Followers need to believe that the rewards they receive are fair for the effort they expend, as well as fair compared to rewards others receive for differing levels of performance. Possibly more important, followers need to believe and trust that the leader will be able to deliver on promised rewards. If these two conditions are not met, followers will lack the motivation to perform at high levels.

Emphasize the positive. Behaviors that are rewarded tend to be repeated while behaviors that are not rewarded, or are punished, tend to not reoccur.[12] Leaders should apply this knowledge by exhibiting a positive attitude and emphasizing the positive. Words of encouragement, recognition, rewards, and similar reinforcers that are tied to follower performance will all aid in motivating exceptional performance.

There are times when you as a leader must punish a follower for dangerous or unethical behavior. Punishment will rarely motivate a follower to improve performance but can be used to end unacceptable behavior. Though excessive use of punishment should be avoided because of the negative effects it has on the organization, leaders must enforce rules and expectations.[13] Punishment and a lack of rewards may help a leader achieve compliance with standards, but those leaders who want exceptional performance from their followers should emphasize the positive in every way possible.

Praise where you can. One of the most effective ways to motivate employees is not through pay or other concrete rewards, but through simple praise. While any feedback on performance is helpful to followers, telling them they are doing things right and are appreciated is particularly effective. Praise addresses a variety of follower needs, aids in boosting self-efficacy, and generally strengthens the relationship between you and your follower. Giving praise is easy and doesn't have a monetary cost.

Giving praise is a simple, three-step process as summarized in Figure 4.1. First, tell the follower what she did correctly; second, tell the follower why what she did is important; and then, encourage the follower to continue doing it.[14]

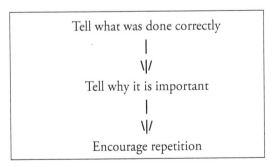

Figure 4.1 Giving praise

Source: Adapted from Lussier and Achua (2016).

While a rule of thumb in Western cultures is to "praise in public; punish in private," leaders who have followers from other cultures may want to both praise and punish in private. In either case, the effect of praise will still be strong.

Positive Expectations Lead to Positive Performance

Understanding what and how followers are motivated is important because it helps explain why they behave the way they do and enables you as the leader to direct the behavior of followers toward the organizations goals. Insight into behavior and motivation helps build positive expectations. As leaders develop relationships with their followers and learn about their backgrounds, needs, and goals, they can use this information to create positive expectations and influence the motivation and behavior of their followers.

By knowing what followers need and understanding how the motivation process works, leaders can develop realistic expectations and clearly communicate performance standards and the rewards available for followers who achieve them. Creating jobs and tasks that provide for growth, group membership, and recognition are integral steps to establishing positive expectations. As you work to help followers develop self-efficacy and trust that their leader can deliver on the promised rewards, your followers will develop positive expectations for themselves and work harder to try to perform at the reward level. Focusing on the positive in relationships, conversations, and rewards will further enhance the positive expectations of followers. Giving praise where it is due is also a powerful motivator.

CHAPTER 5

Communicating to Motivate

Once you have a solid understanding of motivation and the motivation process, you can begin to develop specific strategies to help employees to be motivated. A promising line of research based on Sullivan's **Motivating Language Theory**[1] gives concrete advice for strategic leader–follower communication. Sullivan's original work asserted that a strategic leader with an expanded oral language repertoire would better engage, motivate, build commitment, and create a shared organizational vision with followers.[2]

Results from numerous studies have validated Sullivan's assertions and show significant and positive relationships between leader motivating language (ML) and critical organizational outcomes such as employee innovation, job performance, self-efficacy, job satisfaction, effective decision making, perceived leader effectiveness, and leader communication satisfaction. Research has also identified links between high ML use and lower employee withdrawal behaviors, including absenteeism and intent to turnover.[3] Similarly, written ML has been found to have a positive effect on team creativity in a virtual workplace experimental design.[4] Thus, a leader's use of ML tends to have positive effects whether the messages are written or oral. Research indicates that a 10 percent increase in ML can increase job satisfaction among subordinates by approximately 10 to 12 percent and performance by approximately 2 percent.[5, 6]

Motivating language theory includes four additional assumptions as well that are important to keep in mind:

- Leader language covers most verbal expressions that can occur in leader-to-follower talk.
- Leader messages must be accurately perceived by followers.

- Leader behavior strongly impacts the effect of ML on worker outcomes; if leader language and leader behavior are incongruent, then the effect of leader behavior will dominate. The leader must "walk the talk."
- Leaders are most effective through the regular and appropriate use of all types of ML.[7]

While most any message from the leader to the follower can be perceived as motivating, certain type of messages can be particularly motivating. Followers play a large part in what they consider to be motivating as they must "get" the intended message, and those messages must be congruent with the leader's behavior. Finally, the more often and appropriately you use the three types of ML, the more effective you will be as a leader. Motivating Language Theory proposes that the effectiveness of a leader in using three types of communication with their followers has a significant impact on important organizational outcomes. These three types of communication are direction giving/uncertainty reducing, meaning making/culture explanation, and empathetic communication, as illustrated in Table 5.1.

Why use ML? As mentioned, research indicates that a leader's increased use of the three kinds of ML is associated with a host of positive organizational outcomes, including increased performance, increased follower job satisfaction and self-efficacy, perceived leader communication competence, leader effectiveness, and so on. Thus, the "why" becomes self-evident; using ML helps you become a more effective leader. In more concrete terms, the question becomes, "How can you use ML more effectively?"

Table 5.1 Types of motivating language

Direction-giving/uncertainty-reducing language—explains rules, structures, and values of the culture of an organization.
Meaning-making/culture explanation language—clarifies instructions, clears up confusions, and so on.
Empathetic language—expresses emotions of a leader through shared feelings, praise, criticisms, and so on.

Direction-Giving/Uncertainty-Reducing Language

Direction-giving/uncertainty-reducing language occurs when a leader removes ambiguity or clarifies tasks, goals, or rewards for followers.[8] For instance, when a leader takes the time to explain a complicated reward system to employees, direction-giving language occurs as he explains how to achieve the rewards. Similarly, direction-giving language is being applied when a leader clearly explains a strategic initiative so followers understand the specifics of what needs to be done, how to proceed, and what will be gained as a result of achieving this initiative.[9]

As a leader, your communication with followers should always be clear and concise. There are, however, specific kinds of messages that both leaders and followers recognize as fitting this category. You should practice these and make them a regular part of your conversations with followers:

- **Giving clear directions.** As effective leaders give directions, they stress the performance outcomes and duties expected of their followers. They also make sure that followers get the information that is relevant to their tasks.
- **Providing feedback.** Effective leaders provide positive feedback when followers perform at the expected level or above. Leaders also provide specific feedback on how to improve performance when followers are not performing at the expected level. This feedback should always focus on the things the follower can control, such as behaviors, rather than things followers can't change, such as personalities.
- **Using appropriate message channels.** Effective leaders tailor their messages to fit the individual and the situation. They use words and phrases the followers are sure to understand rather than trying to show off their vocabulary of complex words and sentences. Leaders use the communication media that is most appropriate. While e-mails and texts work well for simple instructions and details, phone or face-to-face messages may be more effective when the leader expects resistance or confusion from followers. For instance, while an e-mail congratulating a follower on a job well done may have a positive

impact on motivation, a face-to-face congratulation offered in the presence of others will typically have a much stronger impact. Many times, an effective leader will use combinations of media, such as following up a face-to-face conversation with an e-mail or memo with more detail.

Meaning-Making/Culture Explanation Language

Meaning-making/culture explanation language conveys organizational mental models and underscores each follower's contribution or purpose as it relates to organizational goals. Meaning-making language can also be informal and symbolic. When leaders through either casual conversations or formal talk help followers interpret the culture and values of an organization, they are engaging in meaning-making communication. Similarly, when leaders tell stories or use metaphors, they are using meaning-making language. For instance, a leader's story of a customer service representative going to extraordinary lengths to satisfy a disappointed customer is an example of meaning-making language. When a leader publicly praises and participates in a charity event such as the local "Dragon Boat Race" supporting cancer survivors, meaning-making messages are conveyed about the importance to the organization of supporting local charities.

Meaning-making or culture explanation messages are particularly important for followers who are new to the organization. They are also important for more seasoned followers when there are major organizational or cultural changes, but are less necessary in times of organizational stability. Messages that inform followers of organizational opportunities for them are important for all, and effective leaders make sure followers hear these messages. Helping followers understand why they need to do something a certain way or carefully follow a policy are examples of using meaning-making language.

The meaning-making messages that leaders should share with new followers include explanations of the culture. For example, as a department head in the business school in a military college, I spent lots of time explaining the military system to new professors who had only worked in more typical colleges and lacked military experience. The military college is a unique culture, and it is important for new faculty to understand how the military and academic systems overlap. Meaning-making messages may include how to fit in as well. For instance, if your software company has a "Silicon Valley laid-back" culture, you might need to talk with your new hire from IBM (a more traditional "dark suit, white shirt formal" kind of company) about how to fit in with colleagues.

Another kind of meaning-making message involves storytelling. It is especially important for new followers to hear both stories about how an individual can be successful in the organization and examples of how individuals have failed in the organization. Of course, tact should be used in relating these stories so the individuals mentioned are not exposed.

Empathetic Language

When you as a leader express humanity to a follower[10] that goes beyond formal boundaries, you are using **empathetic language**. Giving praise, mentioned in the previous chapter, is one example of empathetic language. Empathetic communication is compassionate, showing genuine concern for followers.[11] In the same way, properly delivered criticism by the leader for mistakes or poor performance will translate to the follower as empathetic, though the leader shows disappointment.

Effective leaders use their own and their followers' emotions to their advantage. While it's generally not a good idea for you as a leader to "lose your cool" when upset, letting your followers know how you feel can aid in their motivation. However, it is generally smart to express positive emotions when they fit. Sharing emotions, feelings, praise, and criticism with followers is important to building positive relationships with followers. Of course, it goes without saying that the level of emotion a leader expresses should fit the situation, or the leader will be seen as insincere.

When you spend time talking with followers about nonwork-related issues such as families, vacations, weekend activities, and so on, you help followers realize that you care about them as people, not just as "human resources" necessary to accomplish the organization's goals. In some situations, you may need to spend time with followers discussing how to better deal with their colleagues in the workplace or other difficult people and situations. Doing this not only provides direction but also lets them know that you have relevant experiences similar to their own.

Effective leaders selectively choose the best media for expressing emotions to their followers. Rather than sending an e-mail expressing condolences to a follower who has lost a family member, an effective leader would, whenever possible, do this face-to-face. Likewise, if you are disappointed in a follower's performance, the most effective way to express this is privately one-on-one rather than in a public area. An old rule of thumb is to "praise in public, and punish in private." Additionally, we all acknowledge that a handwritten "thank-you" rather than a typed one has much more impact on the person receiving it.

As discussed in an earlier chapter, effective leaders listen actively to their followers and choose the best environment to do this. Taking the time to listen to your followers as they express emotions will aid in growing those important positive relationships and make followers more willing to try to accomplish the tasks you set for them.

Communicating to Motivate

A leader who regularly and consciously uses the techniques of ML will surely be more effective in his leadership efforts than one who uses them only occasionally. One way to begin to ensure that you are making good use of ML is to start with a self-analysis using the Motivating Language Questionnaire for Leaders (MLQL)[12] found in Appendix 1. Results of the MLQL will provide you with an in-depth look at the kinds of messages a leader might use in motivating followers. An honest self-appraisal will identify the types of messages you are using regularly and those you need to use more often to better motivate your followers. Once you've identified these, you can work to make improvements in your conversations with followers.

What may be more important than how **you** think you are using ML is how much your followers think you are using the three types of motivating messages. To determine this, ask your followers to anonymously complete the Motivating Language Questionnaire (MLQ) found in Appendix 2 and compute average scores for direction-giving, meaning-making, and empathetic language. When you compare these averages to your self-evaluation (your MLQL), you will have a solid idea of where you need to improve.

Some research indicates that male and female followers may interpret some of the types of motivating messages differently (direction giving as meaning making, and vice versa).[13] Additionally, followers with leadership experience as opposed to those without leadership experience may perceive some of the messages differently.[14] However, these different interpretations have little impact on the power of ML to increase performance, job satisfaction, and perceptions of leader effectiveness. In short, the positive impact of ML makes it definitely worth the effort of practicing the technique on a regular basis. Exercises to help you in your practice of ML may be found in Appendix 3.

CHAPTER 6

Leading and Communicating Change

Leading is all about change. In today's work environment, the only constant is change, and whether it's the technological environment or the human environment, the rate of change seems to be increasing at an accelerating pace. The job of a leader is change. You must work to make things better, search for better ways to get things done. According to two experts on the subject, leaders "sometimes have to shake things up. Other times they just have to grab hold of the adversity that surrounds them."[1]

As a leader, when you give directions, influence followers, or set objectives, you are trying to change the organization and the people in it.[2] When you explain the organization's culture to new members or describe changes to your regular followers, you are attempting to change how they interact with each other and with the workplace. When you consciously express emotions to motivate followers, you are trying to change things. Leading is about change, and leading changes in your organization is all about communicating effectively.

Resistance to Change

If the one constant today is change, then something that is almost as inherent is that people resist change. They may resist because they like things to stay the same, to stay where they are comfortable, or out of habit to stay with what they are familiar. Leaders who develop strong relationships with followers can create and manage changes more effectively. While changes may modify the status quo and create stress and discomfort, leaders who develop strong relationships with followers can create and manage changes effectively. Some of the reasons that people resist change are found in Table 6.1

Table 6.1 *Reasons people resist change*

Damage to self-interest

Uncertainty about the change

Questions concerning the potential success of the change

Distrust of leadership or fear of being manipulated

Threat to culture and values

Source: Adapted from Lussier and Achua (2016).

Damage to self-interest. When organizational changes occur, many people fear that their positions, power, and relationships will be harmed. Having to learn new things, to change job duties, and to potentially lose fellow workers or their own positions can create strong reasons to resist changes.

Uncertainty about the change. A lack of information about the change can create uncertainty that is very stressful. Followers who feel uncertain about the future are not likely to support a change.

Questions concerning potential success of the change. Past difficulties or failures can create cynicism and resistance to change. People may also question whether changes are necessary, especially if leaders don't communicate the need for change effectively. This can create an "If it ain't broke, don't fix it" mentality and increase resistance to change.

Distrust of leadership or fear of being manipulated. All of us have heard stories of leaders who have been untruthful or have not told followers the whole truth. We've all known individuals with hidden agendas that could harm the organization or even ourselves. The threat of such a situation, whether real or perceived, can create resistance to change. Likewise, the fear of being manipulated or used can create the same kind of resistance.

Threat to culture and values. When an organization has an entrenched culture and deeply held values, any threat to them can create very strong resistance to change. Significant resistance can result in an organization with a very collegial culture, when a new leader comes in with a vision of moving the organization in a new direction.[3] When I first moved to my current employer almost 30 years ago, the new leader who hired me had a vision of changing the culture from a complete emphasis on teaching and collegiality to a more balanced teaching/research culture. The leader did not do a good job of convincing the long-term faculty of the benefits, and they set up a strong resistance. In fact, of the five new people the leader hired, I was the only one left after only five years. It's taken three successive leaders and 30 years to successfully change our culture.

Any threat to an organization's culture and values can create resistance when people believe in and are comfortable being a part of an organization. For instance, in a company that has made its reputation on personal customer service, the employees may resist a change to e-business and selling on the Internet unless they are convinced that the new way of selling will fit with the current culture and values.

Effective leaders must recognize that resistance to change is real and that it can have a significant impact on their efforts to change an organization. To overcome potential resistance, they must work hard to communicate the reasons for and benefits of the change and keep followers informed. Trust and positive relationships are critical. Effective leaders must develop strategies to deal with resistance to change, strategies to put that change in place, and take steps to make sure that the changes become permanent.

Steps in Leading Change

Change is about people. People only embrace change when the current situation is too painful to bear or the new situation is so enticing that they are drawn to it. This is the same for both individuals trying to break bad habits and organizations trying to make changes in procedures, cultures, or other aspects of the organization. As a leader, you may need to change both individuals and the organization in which they work to implement successful change.

Before you as a leader can lead a change successfully, you must create trust and positive relationships with followers and engage in clear and open communication with them. If you have established positive and trusting relationships with followers, they will be more likely to aid in making a change rather than resisting it. You will also get better answers when you ask questions related to the things that may need changing.

Asking purposeful questions can create interest and focus that will help you identify potential areas for resistance and engage your followers in developing strategies to make the change successful.

An **environmental analysis** (both within and external to the organization) is a plan that can help you identify strengths and weaknesses within the organization as well as threats and opportunities. Such an analysis will also indicate areas where change is needed. You, as the leader, possibly with help from followers, can then develop a vision of a successful future and a strategy for the necessary change using the following steps.

1. **Create a sense of urgency**—It is here that the leader has to communicate the reason why the change must be made along with the reason why the organization and its members should exert all possible energy to making it happen as quickly as possible. Without a sense of urgency, followers are unlikely to work enthusiastically, if at all, to make the change.

   Organizations and their members tend to become complacent and accept the comfortable status quo, especially if it has been successful. This complacency can lead to future failures.[4] The owners of a local independent hardware store that had been very successful over a 30-year period ignored the arrival in town of two new "big-box" hardware stores because of their previous success and reputation. This complacency finally led to near failure and the eventual sale of the business. Had those owners recognized the dangers and felt a sense of urgency, they possibly could have increased customer service, reduced and specialized their inventory, focused on commercial customers, and so on, to create a different niche in the local market, which would have allowed them to continue in business. Because of their complacency, however, the changes they did implement were too little, too late.

   Effective leaders will also question the status quo.[5] You should ask "why" when you hear, "We've always done it that way" as a reason to continue a policy or procedure. Maintaining status quo is a poor reason not to change and can easily contribute to complacency and a lack of urgency to engage in a change that will be beneficial for all.

To overcome complacency among followers, leaders often have to engage in "bold or risky" actions that tend to increase conflict.[6]

This essential sense of urgency needs to be created well before reaching the crisis stage, though it can be challenging to get organizations and people to grasp that a crisis is near and the status quo is unacceptable. One good way to do this is to use hard data that shows that even if the organization is currently successful, the situation can rapidly deteriorate and negative consequences are imminent. If the organization has been successful in the past, you may choose to remove some of the perks that came with the previous success markers. This action can point out how bad the situation will be without the needed change. It would be a minor change, but when a supervisor cuts out the free food at regularly scheduled lunch meetings, it becomes clear that there are financial issues and change is critical. The "bold" moves must fit the situation and the change that is needed, but creating a sense of urgency is paramount to successful change.

2. **Communicate your vision**—As mentioned in Chapter 1, while vision implies the distant future and complexity, it can be as simple and short term as the end result of a new project. A leader's vision should include both a picture of the future and an explanation of why the people involved should work toward that future. A clear vision provides both direction and compelling reasons for going in that direction. This vision also enables people to "get on board" the vehicle for change. An effective vision must be both desirable and feasible. It provides focus for energy and activity, yet leaves enough flexibility to allow the organization to react to unexpected problems.[7]

Most importantly, the vision must be communicated clearly and concisely to followers in a compelling way. If followers can't understand or agree on the importance of your vision for change, they will resist implementing it, and your plan will fail. An effective vision is a mental model shared between leaders, followers, and other organizational entities, which explains and gives direction, meaning, and value to relevant stakeholders. Such a message should also reflect compassion and respect for them.[8] Communicating this vision strategically employs the three previously discussed components of motivating language with both internal followers and other organizational stakeholders. As you work to persuade followers to embrace your vision, you will be best served by a vision that goes beyond facts and appeals to the heart.[9]

Once you have developed the clear, concise, and compelling message that summarizes your vision, you not only need to effectively communicate it to followers, but you also need to frequently repeat the message as a way to overcome the natural tendency toward complacency. Organizations reinforce their vision in a variety of ways including displaying vision posters in their facilities, posting their vision on their websites, and referring often to the vision during meetings. When you refer to the vision, make sure your followers understand the positive benefits of working toward the vision for the organization as well as themselves. When people understand "what's in it for them," they will be less likely to resist and will work toward the vision with enthusiasm.

Using symbols and rituals in promoting the vision can help spur change as well.[10] Posters on facility walls, T-shirts with slogans, and giveaways (pens, flash drives, etc.) can all be used to reinforce and communicate your vision and make the change successful. I witnessed the change from a very combative union atmosphere at one plant to a cooperative atmosphere after the human resources department in conjunction with the marketing department introduced T-shirts and a TV ad campaign that reinforced the idea that workers were what made the company and they were important. Steve Jobs used a very ritualistic technique to introduce new products for Apple, which encouraged workers to get excited about the new products as well as stimulate sales.

3. **Use relationships to help guide the change**—Leaders can rarely make changes by themselves. If you have developed positive relationships with followers, you can enlist them in helping to develop plans and guide the change. Followers are usually more willing to change when they have been involved in identifying what needs to be changed and developing plans for the change.

In many change situations, decisions will need to be made on the spot, and waiting for the leader to arrive will only slow down and possibly derail the change. Empowering followers to make decisions related to the change will both encourage their cooperation and speed up the change. One caveat is that you must make sure the followers have the skills and training to make these decisions. You can also put those followers who have a positive attitude toward the change in positions where they can best help by promoting them or reorganizing[11] so they can become "change champions" and facilitate the change.

4. **Generate small victories**—As you begin to implement a change, you should recognize not only the end goal, but midcourse objectives as well. Celebrating victories along the way undermines cynics and reduces resistance, keeps others on board, and builds momentum.[12]

   Progress breeds additional progress, so recognizing small successes related to the overall goal of the change will encourage your followers to continue to work toward a successful change. When you've had a successful meeting, let followers know you are pleased with the result. When a new procedure has been created, recognize the efforts of your followers. If productivity figures are up but haven't yet met your overall goal, you should make it clear to followers that they are well on their way to overall success. There are many ways to recognize these short-term victories, from making announcements of success at meetings, to providing a Friday pizza lunch, or other more significant rewards.

5. **Anchor changes**—A classic change theory breaks organizational change into three steps, unfreezing, moving, and refreezing in the desired position.[13] One of the most difficult tasks leaders face in making a change is making that change stick.

   As individuals, many of us have gone to seminars and returned to our organization committed to changing the way we do certain things such as vowing to spend more time outside the office finding out what's going on, only to find that after a month or two, we are so busy that we've slid back to the old habit of remaining tethered to our desk. For a variety of reasons, this is common at the organizational level as well. Effective leaders find ways to anchor the changes they implement so that they stay in place, with those changes becoming a new second nature to the organization and their followers. Regularly repeating the vision aids in this process, but making a change permanent may also call for reorganizing, changing job descriptions, implementing reward systems, facilitating learning the new ways of doing things, and creating an environment that emphasizes continuous improvement.[14] When the leader and followers no longer think of the change as a new project or technique, it is probably anchored and has become "the way we do it here."[15]

Leading and Communicating Change

As you work to lead a change, recognize that followers really expect you to "lead" the change. You need to set the example in changing, not only by endorsing the change but also by embracing the change, essentially walking your talk. If the change is to cut expenses by having virtual meetings, you need to make sure that you conduct virtual meetings and do it well. This behavior communicates to your followers that you believe in the change. As noted earlier, when followers are successful in making improvements toward the goal of the change, you should recognize, reward, and celebrate their success. You have to be the head cheerleader in the change process.

One thing leaders should always remember as they lead change is that a change doesn't occur in a vacuum. In fact, in most situations, one change leads to another, and then another. For instance, adding a new product to the product line means sales people have to be trained and informed about how to sell the new product. Moving to a computerized inventory system means that workers will have to learn new skills, and the increase in information may impact a whole range of decisions in the organization. The ripple effect of change must be fully supported with adequate resources and realistic expectations for full implementation. Leaders lead in a dynamic, systemic environment where communication, especially in a change situation, is critical to leader success.

CHAPTER 7

Leading Culturally Diverse Groups

Diversity has changed from something leaders and managers had to deal with to stay out of trouble (lawsuits, etc.) to a major factor in creating organizational opportunities and success. The term *diversity* can be used to refer to differences in age, gender, race, ethnicity, religion, culture, sexual orientation, socioeconomic background, capabilities and disabilities, and a host of other factors.[1] While companies continue with their diversity awareness training, the focus of more successful companies has changed from avoiding the possible negatives of diversity to maximizing the positive benefits. Leaders in these organizations have gone beyond the concept of equal opportunity where people of all cultures are treated the same to recognizing, embracing, and valuing cultural differences among their followers.

Benefits and Costs of Diversity

The simple fact is that diversity is tied to financial and organizational success and the impact it has on today's workplace.[2] At the same time, a more diverse workforce means more potential for internal conflict and difficulties in communication between leaders and followers, so leaders must work hard to maximize the benefits of diversity. Benefits include attracting and retaining the best employees, keeping and gaining market share, enabling more effective decision making, reaching greater levels of innovation, and achieving higher performance.

The costs associated with diversity come from not managing it well or failing to embrace its benefits. Costly barriers to diversity include prejudice, discrimination, stereotyping, and perceptual bias at the individual level, which all have legal implications, but they also can have a significant impact on productivity. These same barriers can exist at the group level. At the institutional level, barriers to diversity include inflexible work hours, lack of entry into informal networks, and in some cases, inaccessible facilities, all of which can make it difficult for women, single parents, people of color, workers with disabilities, and others to reach their potential and maximum productivity. These limiting conditions have indirect costs, including increased conflict between people from different cultures, slower decision making for group decisions, and higher absenteeism and turnover among diverse employees when they are not appreciated for the benefits they bring to the organization.

Understanding Diversity

Your followers likely make up a more diverse group than ever. Today's workforce is vastly different from just a few years ago, as seen in the following statistics in Table 7.1.

Table 7.1 Major shifts in workforce diversity

Generational diversity—For the first time, the workforce is a blend of five different generations of workers (World War II [WWII] generation, baby boomers, Generation X, Generation Y/millennials, and Generation Z [born 1996–present]).[3] From a technological viewpoint, these workers have spanned the development of technology from television, to space travel, to the Internet and cell phones.

Aging workforce—By 2020, the percentage of workers in the 25 to 45-year-old group will decline by approximately 3.2 percent while the age group over 55 years old will increase by 5.7 to 25.2 percent of the workforce,[4] compounding the age issue between entering and veteran workers.

Increase in foreign-born workers—Foreign-born workers (approximately 25 million) make up approximately 16 percent of today's U.S. workforce. By 2030, this number will increase by almost 10 million,[5] making the U.S. workforce even more diverse.

Growth in women in the workforce—There are currently more women than men in the U.S. workforce. Compared to the past, these women are more likely to be full-time workers with more education than their male counterparts. While it is noteworthy that women in the United States fare better economically than women in most other countries, they still are paid about 75 percent of the wages of men in comparable positions, while bearing a disproportionate share of child and household duties.[6] Many working women are heads of single-parent families.

Understanding diversity goes beyond age, race, and gender to include aspects of the different cultures of followers. It is common in today's global business world for leaders to be assigned positions in locations beyond their home country. It is even more common to have followers from various cultural backgrounds, which makes the issue of leading people from different cultures an everyday occurrence.

Culture can be defined in a variety of ways, and the concept is complicated by the many different types of cultures. Simply put, **culture** is that set of beliefs, rules, and values that influence the way an identifiable group of people think, feel, and behave toward similar people and other groups of people.[7,8] The concept of culture applies to national cultures, ethnic cultures, regional cultures, organizational cultures, and team cultures. Cultural awareness can help leaders and followers understand each other and communicate more effectively. Your task as a leader will be to understand how cultural differences impact communication with your followers and to learn to respect and appreciate those differences. Your efforts will be richly rewarded as research indicates that well-managed diversity yields improvements in decision making,[9] innovation,[10] creativity,[11] and performance.[12]

As a leader of diverse followers, you will need to both recognize and appreciate that other people have had experiences different from your own. You also need to understand the complexities of diversity. Not only are there the obvious differences such as race, ethnicity, gender, and so on, but there are secondary differences as well. These may include such differences as levels of education and academic background, marriage and family status, income levels, and a host of other cultural differences. All of these differences will impact how you and your followers perceive each other and the messages you share.

We tend to be ethnocentric, evaluating the behavior of others relative to our own behaviors, values, and beliefs—our cultural background. Thus, we assume that certain behaviors and responses are appropriate or inappropriate based on our own culture's norms. To overcome this limitation, you will need to develop a capacity to be nonjudgmental. It is important to recognize that what is acceptable in one culture may not be acceptable in others, or what one person sees as appropriate may be seen as inappropriate by others. Clear examples of this include differences in meal etiquette, directness and indirectness in business negotiations, levels of formality and informality in superior–subordinate relationships, and the meanings of gestures and other nonverbal behaviors.

Cultural differences often show up as issues in communicating. Examples of common cultural miscues include showing the soles of your shoes in the Middle East, being too direct in negotiations with Asian business colleagues, being on time or early in Latin American countries, and similar mistakes. Learning about the cultures of your followers and the people and places you work in are critical to cultural intelligence and success.

Understanding Cultures

Cultures can be grouped based on their similarities and differences, though these groupings are essentially generalizations about the cultures and people in them. You should be cautious of overgeneralizing your knowledge of different cultures for several reasons.

Cultures change over time, so many of the generalizations mentioned here and elsewhere may no longer apply completely. The impact of the Internet, changing technologies, and increased travel serves to erase some of the cultural differences that existed in the past. Experts also disagree concerning how to classify some nations, and some cultures have not been studied thoroughly. It is also important to remember that members of cultural groups are individuals and do not have exactly the same values, beliefs, or behaviors as others from that culture. Additionally, people within cultural and political/geographic boundaries are not the same.[13] We are seeing evidence of this in the current conflicts in several Middle Eastern countries. Even so, we can still make some useful generalizations about facets of different cultures and people from those cultures.

Research by Geert Hofstede is widely recognized for its ability to help define cultural differences.[14] He identified five facets that distinguish national cultures from one another. Each of these facets is represented on a continuum with opposing values, as illustrated in Table 7.2.

Acceptance of power inequalities. In the United States and most European cultures, there is little recognition of a "ruling class" and of differences in power and social status. Leaders and followers are viewed to a

Table 7.2 Cultural facets

Acceptance of power inequalities
Strong social classes ←------→ Strong equality
Individualism
Individualistic ←-----→ Collectivist
Materialistic/humane orientation
Materialism/Masculine ←----------→ Quality of life/Feminine (caring)
Tolerance for ambiguity
Comfortable with ambiguity ←------→ Dislike ambiguity
Time orientation
Now focus ←----→ Future focus

Source: Hofstede (1993).

large extent as equals, and leaders may try to seem more collegial and less powerful than they are by involving followers in a variety of ways. However, in countries where there is strong acceptance of **power inequalities**, you will find strong social classes and significant differences in power between leaders and followers. Latin countries and Japan are examples of countries where power inequalities are seen as normal. Thus, followers in Mexico may be uncomfortable working with an American leader who wants to operate as a team, seeking advice from followers and involving them in decision making; they may prefer a more authoritarian leader. As the level of acceptance of power inequalities increases, the greater is the fear of disagreeing with the leader and the greater the expectation that the leader will be directive. On the other hand, in more power-equal cultures, workers will feel comfortable disagreeing with the leader and will expect to be involved in decision making.[15] The United States has a considerably power-equal culture, with American workers wanting to be involved in decisions.

Individualism. In individualistic cultures, the focus is on individuals and their needs and goals, whereas collectivist cultures focus on the needs and goals of the group (family, organization, country). Great Britain and Canada are typically labeled as individualistic, while countries such as Greece, Japan, China, and Mexico are labeled as collectivist.[16] The United States is often rated as the most individualistic of all cultures. Followers in **individualistic cultures** typically respond well to individual praise and rewards, while followers from **collectivist cultures** may feel uncomfortable when singled out for praise and rewards and feel more comfortable with team rewards. Likewise, followers in individualistic cultures prefer direct criticism and confrontation, while those from collectivist cultures prefer indirect criticism and more subtle confrontation.

When functioning as a leader in a collectivist culture, you must make sure that ideas appear to come from the group rather than from individuals. You must also consider group norms and values in decision making and involve the group in those decisions.[17] Even within a national culture, you can find organizations that don't "fit the mold." While the U.S. culture is classified as one of the most individualistic, many organizations encourage a collectivist culture within. The emphasis on teams and the concept of treating the employees as "family" are prevalent practices throughout the nation. Thus, as a leader, you will need to apply the concepts of cultural intelligence at the organization level as well as at the national level.

Materialistic/humane orientation. Materialistic cultures emphasize assertiveness and achievement. People in these cultures are motivated by competition and extrinsic rewards, which are often considered masculine traits. At the other end of the continuum are humane cultures that stress values that are often considered feminine. These include quality-of-life issues such as cooperative relationships, camaraderie at work, and overall well-being for all as well as the intrinsic satisfaction that goes with meaningful work.[18] In **materialistic cultures**, traditional male roles typically dominate, whereas in **humane cultures**, there is little difference in power between male and female roles. Scandinavian countries such as Sweden and Norway are seen as some of the most humane cultures, while Japan, Austria, Venezuela, and Guatemala are the most masculine.

The U.S. orientation for materialistic/humane orientation falls near the middle. As a leader in a materialistic culture, you may be expected to be more assertive as a decision maker, relying on logic and facts, whereas in a more humane culture, you will need to focus more on interpersonal relationships and place more emphasis on the welfare of the group. Your humane followers will have more of a "work to live" attitude, while your materialistic followers are likely to have more of a "live to work" attitude.[19] This dichotomy will influence both your communication with followers and the techniques you use to motivate their performance.

Tolerance for ambiguity. People in some cultures are comfortable dealing with unstructured situations and ambiguity, while in other cultures people are less comfortable with ambiguity and prefer situations with a high degree of certainty and structure. Those from cultures with a tolerance for **ambiguity** will likely follow strict codes of conduct and believe in absolute truths, while those from cultures with a high tolerance for ambiguity will typically have a higher tolerance for risk, be less "rule oriented," be more receptive to change, and be more likely to follow their own judgment or common sense rather than rules or regulations.[20] Countries including Greece, Portugal, Belgium, and Japan are considered to have low tolerance for ambiguity. In contrast, the United States, Jamaica, Denmark, Sweden, and Ireland are considered high-tolerance countries[21] where there is a low level of uncertainty avoidance.

Your followers from cultures with a low tolerance for ambiguity are likely more comfortable with leaders who are older and/or have more seniority. These traits are less important in high-tolerance cultures. Those from cultures with a low tolerance for ambiguity will typically prefer clear instructions, follow orders willingly, disapprove of competition between followers, and be more loyal than your high-tolerance followers.[22]

Time orientation. In some cultures, people live in the here and now (short term), while in other cultures, they focus on the future (long term). Cultures with a **short-term time orientation** respect tradition, typically don't engage in significant planning efforts, and are essentially spontaneous. On the other hand, in **long-term time orientation** cultures, people will sacrifice the present for future goals and spend significant efforts in planning for the future. Followers from short-term cultures respond to extrinsic rewards, while followers from long-term cultures are more concerned with intrinsic rewards. Followers from long-term cultures tend to use concrete language, while those from short-term cultures often use more flexible language.[23] Asian countries are associated with long-term orientation. Middle Eastern countries as well as the United States, Canada, and the Philippines are characterized as short-term-oriented cultures.

Leaders of long-term-oriented followers can expect more loyalty and sacrifice for long-term goals. Short-term-oriented cultures will demand more immediate progress. Members of long-term cultures are often strongly motivated by feelings of shame, which can be used to help influence followers to comply with directions from you as the leader.[24]

High- Versus Low-Context Cultures

Another way to view cultures is through the predominant communication style of the culture, that is, how much the context of a message influences the meaning that is taken from that message. In **high-context cultures** including most Asian cultures, people rely on nonverbal signals and other factors to help determine meaning. Age, seniority, position, and reputation are important parts of the message. In **low-context cultures** such as the United States and most of Europe, people focus on the spoken and written message, with nonverbal factors not as important. Thus, in high-context cultures, sometimes what is NOT said may be more important than what is actually spoken or written. American leaders in Asian companies and Asian leaders in American companies have frequently found these differences in culture difficult to deal with.

As a leader in high-context cultures, you will need to work hard to establish relationships, develop trust with followers, and pay careful attention to nonverbal messages. In low-context cultures, personal relationships between people are less important. People tend to rely on oral agreements in high-context cultures and on written, clearly worded agreements in low-context cultures. Leaders in low-context cultures can be direct in their evaluations of and directions to followers. In high-context cultures, leaders should typically be less direct, and orders should sound more like "suggestions."[25]

Subcultures and Mixed Cultures

The most common situation in which leaders encounter cultural and diversity issues is in their everyday work groups. While teams you lead may not include followers from other countries, your team will still be a diverse group with all the benefits and costs that accompany diversity. The concept of cultural understanding can be extended to subcultures as well. For instance, within the American culture, it is safe to say there are a myriad of subcultures that we encounter regularly. People from the Northeast are different from those from the West Coast, who are different from people from the Southeast, who are different from those from the Midwest, and so forth. In the business environment, accountants are different from marketers, who are different from IT specialists, who are different from engineers, and so on. Some of your followers will be married with children, some single parents, some with no partners, and so on. There will be differences in gender and gender orientation, age, experience, and so on.

In the United States, Caucasian women, native Americans, and African Americans tend to prefer a more high-context communication environment than do Caucasian males.[26] Your followers may all be natural citizens of the country but may still represent a mix of ethnic backgrounds, economic situations, family situations, and so on, which will impact how you communicate with and lead them. While these differences might seem slight, they show up in values and behaviors and impact workplace behavior and communication. The more diverse the group, the more challenging and complicated is your effort to adapt your communication and motivation efforts to each individual.

Working with Cultural Diversity

There are several things you can do as a leader to work more effectively with a culturally diverse workforce.

- **Know your own cultural background and biases.** This knowledge is critical to understanding people different from you.
- **Learn the cultural backgrounds of each of your followers and others you work with.** Keep an open mind and be careful not to judge based on your own culture.
- **Create a climate of trust, respect, collaboration, and empathy.** Considering the viewpoints of your followers helps bridge cultural gaps.

- **Listen actively**, especially when you are confused or in doubt about what others are saying.
- **Focus on facts rather than your interpretation of them**, which may be different from that of your followers with different cultural backgrounds.
- **Craft a group culture that combines the assets of each of the cultures in the group.** By reminding your followers and yourself of common goals and the need to adapt to different communication styles and preferences, you can create a unique group culture.

Because of the significant workforce changes, it is more important than ever to develop the cultural intelligence to lead a diverse group of followers. **Cultural intelligence** focuses on a leader's ability to work with and adapt to members of other cultures and can be developed and improved over time with training, experience, and conscious effort.[27] You will need to cultivate your ability to reason and your observation skills to interpret unfamiliar situations in leading people from other cultures and to practice appropriate leadership behaviors. A variety of instruments are available on the Internet (both free and paid), which can help you measure your current level of cultural intelligence and provide insight into developing it further.

CHAPTER 8

Leading Is Communicating: Putting It All Together

As a leader, your most important task is to determine what kinds of actions to take and changes to make, and then to communicate them to your followers and persuade them to action. Quite simply, an effective leader must determine a vision for the future, communicate it to followers, and motivate them to work toward reaching that goal. In even simpler terms, the leader determines an objective and implements plans to achieve it. There are several things a leader can do to increase the probability of success.

Know Yourself

One of the oldest bits of advice for leaders is to "know yourself." You should learn and understand your own values and beliefs and how they impact your leadership style and practices.

Knowing your own personality and communication style and how others react to you is essential, as is knowledge of your strengths and weaknesses in the areas of technical, conceptual, and human skills. The more you know and understand who you are and why you are the person you are, the better you will be able to identify your own strengths and weaknesses as a leader. With this knowledge, you can develop your own plan to develop your weaknesses into strengths while capitalizing on the strengths you have. By recognizing your weaknesses, you can surround yourself with followers who have strengths in the areas where you are not as strong. Further, the better you understand who you are, the easier it will be to understand your followers who are different from you and communicate more effectively with them.

Develop Positive Relationships

Clearly, developing positive relationships with followers is a recurring theme throughout this book, as it is the key to being a successful leader. Followers who understand their leader and what the leader wants to accomplish are most likely to put forth the necessary effort to succeed. If followers know you have their interests at heart, they are more likely to follow in the directions you give. Several suggestions for developing relationships with your followers have been presented in this book.

- *Listening* is critical to developing relationships. In fact, some experts suggest that leaders first listen to followers before directing them.
- Expressing *empathy* with followers helps them to know you understand them and have their interests at heart. Communicating your own values to your followers will aid in their understanding you as well.
- Having an *awareness* of what your own values and beliefs are and of the impact you have on others, especially your followers, is a measure of the emotional intelligence necessary to successful leadership.
- While being *accountable* to yourself and your superiors for your own actions is critical, you should also be accountable to your followers. This mutual accountability helps followers know they can count on you.
- You should build your *team* by fostering positive relationships among your followers as well as with you. When this happens, followers most likely will feel accountable to both you and each other to perform at the highest level.

Following these suggestions will help you develop a strong and committed group of followers who will be willing to exert the effort necessary to achieve the vision or objective you have set for them.

Build trust. The suggestions just discussed lay the groundwork for positive relationships. To maintain those relationships, you will need to build and sustain trust with your followers. Trust is a complex concept that includes five components: *integrity, consistency, competence, loyalty,* and *openness.* Trust is also a two-way concept. Not only do your followers have to trust you, but they also need to know that you trust them because they exhibit these same five components in their work and relationships with you and each other.

Integrity involves being honest and doing the right thing all the time, not only when your superiors and followers see you, but even when no one is looking. Followers will only trust a leader who is honest. Similarly, followers will not trust a leader who is inconsistent, doing one thing this time, and another the next.

Consistency lets followers know what to expect from you. Effective leaders demonstrate their *competence* regularly, letting followers know that the leader knows what and how things should be done.

Effective leaders are *loyal* to the organization, themselves, and to their followers. Effective leaders will go to bat for followers who make mistakes and protect them from unnecessary abuse from people outside the group.

As mentioned earlier, effective leaders rarely hold back information from their followers. By being *open* about what is happening in the organization, followers can make effective decisions of their own and make your job as the leader less difficult.

Lead by example. When you demonstrate the five components of trust to your followers, you are already *leading by example.* While this phrase is overworked in the leadership literature and may seem trite, it is possibly one of the most important things you can do to lead effectively. Followers will not eagerly follow a leader who says one thing and does another. Nor will they go above and beyond for a leader who asks them to do something that the leader would not do. Many times your actions will speak louder than your words, so you should always try to "model the way" for your followers.

Get help to check the vision. To make sure that the objective is clear and compelling, you should discuss it with your mentors to make sure they both understand it and agree that it is achievable. Likewise, you could discuss your vision with the most influential of your followers to see whether they will buy into your objective since it's your followers who will be doing most of the work toward achieving it. Clearly, the larger your in-group, the better the chance is that they will help you achieve your objective. When you have developed strong positive relationships with your followers, they will be able to share your vision as their own.

Once you are satisfied that the vision you will communicate to your followers is clear and compelling, you should choose the right way to communicate it. Sometimes that will be in individual meetings, sometimes in small groups, and at times to all your followers at once. If at all possible, face-to-face conversations should be used first, repeating the message as necessary through written or electronic media. Regardless of the medium you choose, you should continue to communicate the vision until it becomes a reality.

Use Motivation as Your Key to Success

Effective leaders are able to lead because they can influence their followers to act to accomplish the goals set by the organization and the leader. Leaders do this through personal relationships—by knowing and understanding who their followers are as individuals and what they need and want from their jobs and from life. Leaders influence their followers by building positive expectations and applying the appropriate communication techniques to motivate followers to action.

Build positive expectations. Effective leaders make sure their followers understand their assigned tasks and responsibilities, are well trained, and have the resources necessary to accomplish them. Well-equipped followers who know these things will feel confident that they can succeed. Furthermore, when you clearly communicate that by completing their assigned tasks they will receive rewards that they value, their motivation will be stronger and their efforts greater. Providing praise and positive feedback during and after the tasks are complete also provides motivation for the present and reinforcement for the future.

Use motivating language. As we have discussed in several places throughout this book, effective leaders give clear directions. One of the key issues is determining how much direction to give as this will vary depending on how much knowledge and experience your followers have. It is important to give enough direction but to avoid overdoing it and micromanaging your followers. When new situations develop or new followers come on board, it is important to make sure followers understand the implications of the situation. Similarly, it is important for you as a leader to help new followers understand the culture of your organization.

While traditional "pregame pep talks" and "chewing outs" should typically be avoided, effective leaders surely let their followers know how they feel. Likewise, effective leaders let followers know that they understand them and their feelings.

Empower Your Followers and Involve Others

In today's organizations, leading is a team effort. The role of team leader has become more of a coaching/facilitating task than one of directing activities of individuals. As followers have become more educated, experienced, and individualistic, many of them seek to become leaders themselves. At the same time, tasks in most organizations have become more complex.

Effective leaders take advantage of capable followers by empowering them to make decisions that were once the prerogative of the leader alone. Empowering followers gives you more time to focus on the future, making your job less difficult and making both you and your followers more productive.

Good leaders don't want their organization to slow down or stop when they are not there. Empowering followers makes your organization effective even when you're not on the scene and helps develop new leaders who will be needed as your organization grows and changes.

Lead Change

All leadership is about change; however, there are times when changes are very significant. When leading such a change, you need to be sure to publically embrace the change and create a sense of urgency among your followers. When your followers know you are wholeheartedly moving toward the new end product at full speed, they are more likely to join the effort to ensure the change. Celebrating small victories on the path to the end state of the change will reinforce both your own and your followers' efforts in that direction. Finally, one of the most difficult parts of leading a significant change effort is to make sure that the change sticks. You need to continually reiterate the new vision of where you are leading the unit or organization. This will help reinforce the new way that "we do things here" and that followers believe in and they will be committed to making the change stick.

Lead Effectively in a Diverse World

Effective leaders recognize that the people in their organizations today and in the future are more diverse than ever and take advantage of that diversity while dealing with the inevitable issues that come with it. They recognize the most obvious elements of diversity such as race and gender, but also the more subtle differences among their followers. To take advantage of diversity, leaders work hard to listen to their followers, develop trust with them, and encourage collaboration.

Practice Effective Leading

While some people may be "natural" leaders, most are not. All of us can become more effective leaders through practice, and you can learn to lead by being an exemplary follower. Such followers manage themselves, not waiting for direction from leaders, and are engaged in and committed to the organization and its objectives. When you show competence, effort, and enthusiasm as a follower, you will be of greater help to your leader and able to apply these same behaviors when you are in a leadership position. Exemplary followers also exhibit integrity and are willing to show courage to provide feedback when the leader is drifting from the objective.

Effective leaders make mistakes, but learn from them. You should regularly assess your leadership efforts, recognizing the efforts that were effective and those that did not go as planned. Learn from your mistakes and determine how you can do things better in the future.

Effective leaders take action, are committed to achieving their vision and objectives, and are competent and enthusiastic. They know themselves and their followers and create positive relationships. They treat their followers with respect, communicating openly and frequently, and work hard to motivate them. Finally, effective leaders hold both themselves and their followers accountable.

APPENDIX 1

Motivating Language Questionnaire for Leaders (MLQL)

Motivating Language Questionnaire for Leaders

The examples below show different ways you might talk to your followers. Please circle the answer that best matches your conversational style. Be sure to mark only one answer for each question.

Always (A)   Often (O)   Sometimes (S)   Rarely (R)   Never (N)

1. Do I provide my followers with positive feedback when they do a good job in performing organizationally relevant tasks?   A O S R N

2. Do I provide my followers with feedback on how to improve their performance when they are not performing at the desired level?   A O S R N

3. Do I clearly explain to my followers what is expected from them in their job duties?   A O S R N

4. Do I provide my followers with the relevant organizational information needed to perform their jobs?   A O S R N

5. Do I tailor my performance feedback communication to maximize each follower's understanding?   A O S R N

6. Do I use the communication media that are most effective for providing performance direction and feedback?   A O S R N

7. Do I tailor my performance communication so it is more suitable for a given task?   A O S R N

8. Do I spend time talking with my followers about nonwork-related issues?   A O S R N

9. Do I give feedback to my followers in ways that validate their own feelings?   A O S R N

10. Do I talk to my followers about how to better deal with their colleagues in the workplace?   A O S R N

11. Do I let my followers know when I have had relevant experiences similar to their own?   A O S R N

12. Do I show my followers that I am willing to listen to their concerns?   A O S R N

13. Do I use the most appropriate media for expressing my ideas and feelings?   A O S R N

14. Do I show more or less empathy as is appropriate for a given situation?   A O S R N

15. Do I tell my followers about organizational opportunities for them?   A O S R N

16. Do I tell my followers stories about people who have been successful in the organization?   A O S R N

17. Do I tell my followers stories about people who have failed in the organization?   A O S R N

18. Do I provide new followers with information about the organization's culture?   A O S R N

19. Do I tell my followers what they need to do to fit into the organization's culture?   A O S R N

20. Do I tell established followers about how to succeed in the organization's culture?   A O S R N

21. Do I provide followers with cultural information that is relevant to their jobs?   A O S R N

Scoring

For each question, give yourself 4 for each A circled, 3 for each O circled, 2 for each S circled, 1 for each R circled, and 0 for each N circled.

Direction giving: Add your scores for questions 1 to 7. Then divide by 7.
Meaning making: Add your scores for questions 15 to 21. Then divide by 7.
Empathetic: Add your scores for questions 8 to 14. Then divide by 7.

Average scores:
3 to 4: You're doing a good job.
2 to 3: You should work on this.
Below 2: You need serious work here.

APPENDIX 2

Motivating Language Questionnaire (MLQ)

To Be Used by Followers

Motivating Language Questionnaire[1]

The examples below show different ways that your boss might talk to you. Please choose the answer that best matches your own perceptions. Be sure to mark only one answer for each question. The results of your questionnaire are anonymous and will only be shared with your leader in a summary table without names.

Very little	(VL)
Little	(L)
Some	(S)
A lot	(A)
A whole lot	(WL)

Directions

(1) Gives me useful explanations of what needs to be done in my work. VL L S A WL

(2) Offers me helpful directions on how to do my job. VL L S A WL

(3) Provides me with easily understandable instructions about my work. VL L S A WL

(4) Offers me helpful advice on how to improve my work. VL L S A WL

(5) Gives me good definitions on what I must do in order to receive rewards. VL L S A WL

(6) Gives me clear instructions about solving job-related problems. VL L S A WL

(7) Offers me specific information on how I am evaluated.   VL L S A WL

(8) Provides me with helpful information about upcoming changes   VL L S A WL
     affecting my work.

(9) Provides me with helpful information about past changes affecting   VL L S A WL
     my work.

(10) Shares news with me about organizational achievements and   VL L S A WL
     organizational financial status.

Empathy

(11) Gives me praise for my good work.   VL L S A WL

(12) Shows me encouragement for my work efforts.   VL L S A WL

(13) Shows concern about my job satisfaction.   VL L S A WL

(14) Expresses his/her support for my professional development.   VL L S A WL

(15) Asks me about my professional well-being.   VL L S A WL

(16) Shows trust in me.   VL L S A WL

Meaning

(17) Tells me stories about key events in the organization's past.   VL L S A WL

(18) Gives me useful information that I couldn't get through official   VL L S A WL
     channels.

(19) Tells me stories about people who are admired in my   VL L S A WL
     organization.

(20) Tells me stories about people who have worked hard in this   VL L S A WL
     organization.

(21) Offers me advice on how to behave at the organization's social   VL L S A WL
     gatherings.

(22) Offers me advice about how to "fit in" with other members of   VL L S A WL
     this organization.

(23) Tells me stories about people who have been rewarded by this   VL L S A WL
     organization.

(24) Tells me stories about people who have left this organization.   VL L S A WL

For Leader Only—Scoring Directions

To score individual questionnaires:

Very little	(VL)	= 0
Little	(L)	= 1
Some	(S)	= 2
A lot	(A)	= 3
A whole lot	(WL)	= 4

1. Direction giving: Add scores for questions 1 to 10, then divide by 10
2. Empathetic: Add scores for questions 11 to 16, then divide by 6
3. Meaning making: Add scores for questions 17 to 24, then divide by 8

Average the individual scores for each of the three types of motivating language (direction giving, meaning making, and empathetic). Compare these scores with your own Motivating Language Questionnaire for Leaders (MLQL) scores and look for differences of +/− 1.0 or more where followers rated you lower, as areas to work on improving.

APPENDIX 3

Motivating Language Exercises

Motivating Language Role-Playing Scenarios

These exercises are designed both for small groups of three and as individual exercises.[1] The group exercises are done face-to-face, while the individual exercises may be approached as written exercises or just as thought-provoking exercises that will better prepare you for situations in which you can utilize motivating language to be a more effective leader. You may also use the group scenarios as individual exercises if you are alone, to practice how you would approach the situation as the leader, then consider how the follower might react to your message.

Direction-Giving Language Exercises

Group Exercises

Instructions for Group Exercises

Use the following steps for each scenario in your group of three. All three participants can view the scenario to understand the context of the situation.

1. Groups of three: Decide who will serve as leader, follower, and observer.
2. Leader and follower enact the scenario.
3. Observer notes interaction to see whether leader engages in motivating language.
4. Observer gives constructive feedback on improving motivating language.
5. Rotate positions and engage in the next scenario, repeating steps 1 to 4.

Scenario 1

Give directions to a new employee concerning how procedures are different in your firm from other firms where the employee may have worked. For instance, your firm is very formal and relies heavily on written documentation, while several of your competitors are much more casual about procedures. Similarly, you can assume the reverse, and your firm is much more informal than others.

Scenario 2

A follower has come to you asking for further explanation on how to complete a project (select one). The follower has read and heard the instructions but is still confused. Give the follower verbal instructions to make sure he or she understands the project.

Scenario 3

Choose any of the following brief scenarios and respond in a way that will motivate your follower.

1. Explain to a new hire what he/she needs to do to make sure to receive a reward (bonus, recognition, promotion, etc.) for good work.
2. One of your followers has just completed a task on time and on budget. Give that follower feedback on his/her performance.
3. One of your direct reports botched a presentation to top management because he/she didn't prepare well enough. Give the person feedback on his/her performance, which will motivate him/her to be more prepared in the future.

Scenario 4

Give your follower an 8½" × 11" sheet of paper. Turn away from your follower to simulate a phone conversation. Now give the follower directions for making a paper airplane with the sheet of paper. When the task is complete, explore with the follower and observer how you could have been more clear and complete in your directions.

Individual Exercises

Instructions for Individual Exercises

Provide a written answer to any of the following exercises, then review your answer several days later, possibly with a coworker. If there isn't time to do this, spend a few minutes assessing the situation and determining how you would address it.

Scenario 1

Select a task that one of your followers would typically complete, for instance, your followers may have to record their daily expenses when they are out of the office for work. Develop a set of directions to give to a follower who has just been promoted in your department who has not traveled as part of work before. After you've completed the directions, have someone review them to see if your directions are clear.

Scenario 2

The annual performance appraisal for a follower is six months away, but you see performance slipping. How would you communicate your concerns to the follower? What would your message include?

Scenario 3

Think about a situation where your leader gave you directions (orally, in writing, or electronically) that were unclear or confusing and you were demotivated. What would have been a better way for the leader to have given the directions?

Meaning-Making Language Exercises

Group Exercises

Instructions for Group Exercises

Use the following steps for each scenario in your group of three. All three participants can view the scenario to understand the context of the situation.

1. Groups of three: Decide who will serve as leader, follower, and observer.
2. Leader and follower enact the scenario.
3. Observer notes interaction to see whether leader engages in motivating language.
4. Observer gives constructive feedback on improving motivating language.
5. Rotate positions and engage in the next scenario, repeating steps 1 to 4.

Scenario 1

Tell a five-minute story about something that happened in your firm that would help a new employee understand how you do things. For example, an employee was in an auto accident and missed work for several days and other people worked hard to cover for the employee with customers.

Scenario 2

The company Christmas party is coming up next week. Give your newest hire some advice about what he/she should do at the party.

Scenario 3

You've just hired a new employee from the local college. The individual has very little work experience. In a few minutes, explain the work culture of your organization so the new employee will understand expectations, such as the CEO of the company, who is very organized, likes to see uncluttered, almost empty, desks after employees leave at the end of the day.

Scenario 4

Create a story you would tell a new employee about someone in your company who has not done well (poor performance and appropriate negative consequences from this poor performance). Use this story to motivate the new employee.

Scenario 5

One of your followers has just had a conflict with a coworker. You've had a similar experience with someone in the past. Share your experience with your follower to help him/her understand how to deal with the situation.

Individual Exercises

Instructions for Individual Exercises

Provide a written answer to the following exercises, then review your answer several days later, possibly with a coworker. If there isn't time to do this, spend a few minutes assessing the situation and determining how you would address it.

Scenario 1

You are talking to a newly hired worker in your area and you are telling this person about people who have done well at your company. Come up with one (brief) story about someone who has succeeded (performed well and been rewarded for his/her performance). Think about how you would tell the newly hired worker so this story would motivate him/her.

Scenario 2

Think about how the culture of your department could be changed to be more motivating. Now, take the role of a new department head who wants to make these changes. Describe to the current employees why and how you want the culture to change.

Empathetic Language Exercises

Group Exercises

Instructions for Group Exercises

Use the following steps for each scenario in your group of three. All three participants can view the scenario to understand the context of the situation.

1. Groups of three: Decide who will serve as leader, follower, and observer.
2. Leader and follower enact the scenario.
3. Observer notes interaction to see whether leader engages in motivating language.
4. Observer gives constructive feedback on improving motivating language.
5. Rotate positions and engage in the next scenario, repeating steps 1 to 4.

Scenario 1

A new employee handled a difficult situation with an important client very effectively, smoothing over a potential conflict that could have damaged the relationship with the client. You've decided to let the employee know how you feel about his/her performance.

Scenario 2

A follower has done an outstanding job on an assignment (let's say, the follower has used a very creative approach in writing a memo giving instructions for some task). How would you respond?

Scenario 3

You are the regional manager of a retail furniture company. You've been helping in the management and leadership development of three assistant store managers.

- One of the assistants is being promoted to store manager at a prime store. Let that assistant know the good news in such a way that he/she will remain highly motivated.
- The second assistant is being promoted to store manager of a store that has had major problems. She really wanted the prime store because of transportation issues and you know she feels extra pressure to perform in this situation that is less than ideal. Let her know the decision in a way that will keep her motivation high.

- The third assistant also expected to be promoted but will remain an assistant until the next round of promotions. Let him know the disappointing news in a way that will keep his motivation high.

Scenario 4

One of your followers has a sick relative whose illness requires your follower to help out, and he/she wants to spend more time working away from the office. He/she has come to you to talk about this. Listen carefully to the follower's explanation before you respond.

Scenario 5

Let your follower know there is a position coming up in another department for which he/she is very qualified and will do a good job. You hate to lose him/her.

Individual Exercises

Provide a written answer to any of the following exercises, then review your answer several days later, possibly with a coworker. If there isn't time to do this, spend a few minutes assessing the situation and determining how you would address it.

Scenario 1

Think about an incident you experienced in which your supervisor/leader could have used empathetic language but did not, and it demotivated you. Think of three ways that your supervisor could have used empathetic language to motivate you.

Scenario 2

One of your followers has come to you with worries about the layoff that happened yesterday to several coworkers. How would you respond to deal with his/her worries and keep him/her motivated?

Scenario 3

You are a branch manager of a midsized bank. Corporate just announced a merger in which your bank was taken over by another, larger bank. Develop an outline of the topics and messages you would use in a meeting with your followers, telling them about the merger. Though there is much uncertainty, you must keep them motivated.

Notes

Chapter 1

1. Conger (1991).
2. Baldoni (2003).
3. Mayfield and Mayfield (2013).
4. Burns (1978).
5. Yukl (2010).
6. Bennis and Nanus (1985).
7. Simmons and Sharbrough (2013).
8. Hackman and Johnson (2013).
9. Sharbrough, Simmons, and Cantrill (2006).
10. Kotter (1990).
11. Conger (1991).
12. Kotter (1990).
13. Conger (1991).

Chapter 2

1. Northouse (2016).
2. Mayfield and Mayfield (2009b).
3. Northouse (2013).
4. Hackman and Johnson (2013).
5. Lussier and Achua (2016).
6. Northouse (2013).
7. Northouse (2016).
8. Neubert and Dyck (2014).
9. Leman and Pentak (2004).

Chapter 3

1. Lussier and Achua (2016).
2. Lussier and Achua (2016).
3. Fielding (2006).
4. Floyd (1985).

5. Nahavandi et al. (2015).
6. O'Rourke (2010).
7. O'Rourke (2010).
8. O'Rourke (2010).
9. Fielding (2006).

Chapter 4

1. Fielding (2006).
2. Kinicki and Kreitner (2013).
3. George and Jones (2012).
4. Nahavandi et al. (2015).
5. Neubert and Dyck (2014).
6. Defoe (1719).
7. George and Jones (2012).
8. Lussier and Achua (2016).
9. Lussier and Achua (2016).
10. Kinicki and Kreitner (2013).
11. George and Jones (2012).
12. Lussier and Achua (2016).
13. Neubert and Dyck (2014).
14. Lussier and Achua (2016).

Chapter 5

1. Sullivan (1988).
2. Mayfield, Mayfield, and Sharbrough (2015).
3. Mayfield, Mayfield, and Sharbrough (2015).
4. Wang et al. (2009).
5. Mayfield and Mayfield (2002).
6. Sharbrough, Simmons, and Cantrill (2006).
7. Mayfield and Mayfield (2012).
8. Mayfield, Mayfield, and Sharbrough (2015).
9. Simmons and Sharbrough (2013).
10. Sullivan (1988).
11. Miller (2013).
12. Sharbrough, Riggle, and Simmons (2013).
13. Sharbrough and Simmons (2009).
14. Simmons and Sharbrough (2013).

Chapter 6

1. Kouzes and Posner (2007).
2. Lussier and Achua (2016).
3. Lussier and Achua (2016).
4. Kotter (1996).
5. Kouzes and Posner (2007).
6. Kotter (1996).
7. Mayfield, Mayfield, and Sharbrough (2015).
8. Neubert and Dyck (2014).
9. Neubert and Dyck (2014).
10. Kotter (1996).
11. Neubert and Dyck (2014).
12. Neubert and Dyck (2014).
13. Robbins and Judge (2015).
14. Robbins and Judge (2015).
15. Anderson (2015).

Chapter 7

1. George and Jones (2012).
2. Cardon (2014).
3. Levitt (2015).
4. Working in America (2013).
5. Working in America (2013).
6. O'Rourke (2010).
7. George and Jones (2012).
8. Cardon (2014).
9. Cardon (2014).
10. Page (2007).
11. McLeod, Lobel, and Cox (1996).
12. Watson, Kumar, and Michaelson (1993).
13. Hackman and Johnson (2013).
14. Hofstede (1993).
15. Hackman and Johnson (2013).
16. Lussier and Achua (2016).
17. Hackman and Johnson (2013).
18. Neubert and Dyck (2014).
19. Hackman and Johnson (2013).
20. Robbins and Judge (2015).

21. Hackman and Johnson (2013).
22. Hackman and Johnson (2013).
23. Cardon (2014).
24. Hackman and Johnson (2013).
25. Robbins and Judge (2015).
26. Daft (2016).
27. Daft (2016).

Appendix 2

1. Original questionnaire from Mayfield, Mayfield, and Kopf, 1998. Scoring developed by Sharbrough.

Appendix 3

1. Several of these scenarios have been developed from the work of Jackie and Milton Mayfield.

Bibliography

Anderon, D.L. 2015. *Organization Development: The Process of Leading Organizational change.* Thousand Oaks, CA: Sage.

Baldoni, J. 2003. *Great Communication secrets of Great Leaders.* New York, NY: McGraw-Hill.

Bennis, W., and B. Nanus. 1985. *Leaders: The Strategies for Taking Charge.* New York, NY: Harper & Row.

Burns, J.M. 1978. *Leadership.* New York, NY: Harper & Row.

Cardon, P.W. 2014. *Business Communication: Developing Leaders for a Networked World.* New York, NY: McGraw-Hill Irwin.

Conger, J. 1991. "Inspiring Others: The Language of Leadership." *Academy of Management Executive 5,* no. 1, pp. 31–45.

Daft, R.L. 2016. *Management.* 12th ed. Boston: Cengage Learning.

Defoe, Daniel. 1998. *Robinson Crusoe.* Mineola, NY: Dover Publications, Inc.

Fielding, M. 2006. *Effective Communication Is Organizations.* 3rd ed. Cape Town, South Africa: Juta.

Floyd, J.J. 1985. *Listening: A Practical Approach.* Glenview, IL: Scott Foresman.

George, J.M., and G.R. Jones. 2012. *Understanding and Managing Organizational Behavior.* 6th ed. Upper Saddle River, NJ: Prentice Hall.

Hackman, M.Z., and C.E. Johnson. 2013. *Leadership: A Communication Perspective.* 6th ed. Long Grove, IL: Waveland Press.

Hofstede, G. 1993, February. "Cultural Constraints in Management Theories." *Academy of Mangement Executive 7,* no. 1, pp. 81–94.

Kinicki, R., and A. Kreitner. 2013. *Organizational Behavior.* 10th ed. New York. McGraw-Hill/Irwin

Kotter, J.P. 1990, May-June. "What Leaders Really Do." *Harvard Business Review,* pp. 85–97.

Kouzes, J.M., and B.Z. Posner. 2007. *The Leadership Challenge.* 4th ed. San Francisco: Jossey Bass.

Leman, K., and B. Pentak. 2004. *The Way of the Shepherd: Seven Secrets to Managing Productive People.* Grand Rapids, MI: Zondervan.

Levitt, A. 2015, March 29. "Make Way for Generation Z." *New York Times.* Retrieved from www. nytimes.com/2015/03/29/jobs/make way for generation z.html?r=0

Lussier, R.N., and C.F. Achua. 2016. *Leadership: Theory, Application, and Skill development.* 6th ed. Mason, OH: South-Western/Cengage.

Mayfield, J., M. Mayfield, and J. Kopf. 1998. "The Effects of Leader Motivating Language on Subordinate Performance and Satisfaction." *Human Resource Management 37,* nos. 3–4, pp. 235–48.

Mayfield, J., and M. Mayfield. 2002. Leader communication strategies: Critical paths to improving employee commitment. *American Business Review,* 20, 89–94.

Mayfield, J., and M. Mayfield. 2009. "The Role of Leader Motivating Language in Employee Absenteeism." *Journal of Business Communication 46,* no. 4, pp. 455–79.

Mayfield, J., and M. Mayfield. 2012. "The Relationship Between Leader Motivating Language and Self-Efficacy: A Partial Least Squares Model Analysis." *Journal of Business Communication 48,* no. 4, pp. 357–76.

Mayfield, J., M. Mayfield, and W. Sharbrough. 2015. "Strategic Vision and Values in Top Leaders' Communications: Motivating Language at a Higher Level." *International Journal of Business Communication 51,* no. 1, pp. 97–121.

McLeod, P.L., S.A. Lobel, and T.H. Cox. 1996. "Ethnic Diversity and Creativity in Small Groups." *Small Group Research 27,* no. 2, pp. 248–64.

Miller, K. 2013. "Organizational Emotions and Compassion at Work." In *The SAGE Handbook of Organizational Communication: Advances in Theory, Research, and Methods,* eds. L.L. Putnam and D.K. Mumby, 569–87. 3rd ed. Thousand Oaks, CA: Sage.

Neubert, M.J., and B. Dyck. 2014. *Organizational Behavior.* Hoboken, NJ: John Wiley and Sons.

Nahavandi, A., R. Denhardt, J. Denhardt, and M. Aristigueta. 2015. *Organizational Behavior.* Los Angeles, CA: Sage.

Northouse, P.G. 2016. *Leadership: Theory and Practice.* 7th ed. Los Angeles, CA: Sage.

O'Rourke, J.S. 2010. *Management Communication: A Case-Analysis Approach.* 4th ed. Upper Saddle River, NJ: Prentice Hall.

Page, S. 2007. "Diversity Powers Innovation." Center for American Progress, January 26. Retrieved from www.americanprogress.org/issues/2007/01/diversity_powers_innovation.htm

Perkins, D.N.T. 2012. *Leading at the Edge.* 2nd ed. New York, NY: American Management Association.

Robbins, S.P., and T.A. Judge. 2015. *Organizational Behavior.* 16th ed. Boston: Pearson.

Roebuck, D.B. 2012. *Communication Strategies for Today's Managerial Leader.* New York, NY: Business Expert Press.

Rost, J.C. 1991. *Leadership for the Twenty-First Century.* New York, NY: Praeger.

Sharbrough, W., R. Riggle, and S. Simmons. 2013, February. "Analyzing Motivating Language: A Leader Self-Report Study." A paper presented at the joint conference of the Southeast and Midwest Regions of the Association for Business Communication, Louisville, KY.

Sharbrough, W.C., and S. Simmons. 2009, February. "An Analysis of Gender Differences in Leader-Worker Communication." In *Proceedings of the Southeastern Regional Convention of the Decision Sciences Institute*, pp. 529–45. Charleston, SC.

Sharbrough, W., S. Simmons, and D. Cantrill. 2006. "Motivating Language in Industry." *Journal of Business Communication 43*, no. 4, pp. 322–43.

Simmons, S., and W.C. Sharbrough. 2013. "An Analysis of Leader and Subordinate Perceptions of Motivating Language." *Journal of Leadership, Accountability and Ethics 10*, no. 3, pp. 11–27.

Sharbrough, W.C. October, 2011. "Vision Without Implementation Is Only Hallucination: The Importance of Communication to Effective Leadership. Unpublished presentation." *The Association for Business Communication International Conference*, Montreal.

Sullivan, J.J. 1988. "Three Roles of Language in Motivation Theory." *Academy of Management Review 13*, no. 1, pp. 104–15.

Walker, R. 2015. *Strategic Management Communication for Leaders*. 3rd ed. Mason, OH: Cengage.

Wang, C.W., C.T. Hsieh, K.T. Fan, and M. Menefee. 2009. "Impact of Motivating Language on Team Creativity Performance." *Journal of Computer Information Systems 19*, no. 1, pp. 133–40.

Watson, W.E., K. Kumar, and L.K. Michaelsen. 1993. "Cultural Diversity's Impact on Interaction Process and Performance: Comparing Homogeneous and Diverse Task Groups." *Academy of Management Journal 36*, no. 3, pp. 590–602.

Williams, C. 2007. *Effective Leadership*. 7th ed. Waco, TX: LTrek.

Working in America: Overview of the Immigrant Workforce in the United States. 2013. Retrieved from www.aspenwsi.org/wordpress/wp-content/uploads/Fact-Sheet-Foreign-Born-Workforce.pdf

Yukl, G. 2013. *Leadership in Organizations*. 7th ed. Upper Saddle River, NJ: Prentice Hall.

Index

OTHER TITLES IN OUR CORPORATE COMMUNICATION COLLECTION

Debbie DuFrene, Stephen F. Austin State University, Editor

- *Essential Communications Skills for Managers, Volume I: A Practical Guide for Communicating Effectively With All People in All Situations* by Walter St. John and Ben Haskell
- *Essential Communications Skills for Managers, Volume II: A Practical Guide for Communicating Effectively With All People in All Situations* by Walter St. John and Ben Haskell
- *Public Speaking Kaleidoscope* by Rakesh Godhwani
- *The Presentation Book for Senior Managers: An Essential Step by Step Guide to Structuring and Delivering Effective Speeches* by Jay Surti
- *How to Write Brilliant Business Blogs, Volume I: The Skills and Techniques You Need* by Suzan St. Maur
- *How to Write Brilliant Business Blogs, Volume II: What to Write About* by Suzan St. Maur
- *Managerial Communication and the Brain: Applying Neuroscience to Leadership Practices* by Dirk Remley
- *Producing Written and Oral Business Reports: Formatting, Illustrating, and Presenting* by Dorinda Clippinger

Announcing the Business Expert Press Digital Library

Concise e-books business students need for classroom and research

This book can also be purchased in an e-book collection by your library as

- a one-time purchase,
- that is owned forever,
- allows for simultaneous readers,
- has no restrictions on printing, and
- can be downloaded as PDFs from within the library community.

Our digital library collections are a great solution to beat the rising cost of textbooks. E-books can be loaded into their course management systems or onto students' e-book readers.
The **Business Expert Press** digital libraries are very affordable, with no obligation to buy in future years. For more information, please visit **www.businessexpertpress.com/librarians**. To set up a trial in the United States, please email **sales@businessexpertpress.com**.